Crying Tiger
Thai Recipes from the Heart

Supatra Johnson
(สุพัตรา จอร์นสัน)

Photographs by Randall Johnson

Jasmine Market™

Saint Paul, MN.

Copyright ©2004

All rights reserved. No part of this publication may be reproduced, stored in a retreival system or transmitted in any form or by any means electronic, mechanical, photocopying, recording or otherwise, without the prior written permission of the publisher.

Published by
Jasmine Market™
14050 Pilot Knob Rd Suite 140-111
Saint Paul, MN. 55124

Library of Congress Cataloging-in-Publication Data
has been applied for.

International Standard Book Number (ISBN)
0-9742768-0-4

Printed in the United States of America

1st Printing

Acknowledgements

I would like to thank my mom, Saphanthong Khommuangpak, for teaching me everything she knows about cooking, especially how to make Som Tum so spicy it will take your breath away. Thanks to Chef Le Tung at Porn Isaan Restaurant for giving me a chance to learn some of the secrets of Thai cooking! A big thank you to Khun Suchat Chomprayoon, the owner of Porn Isaan Restaurant in Bangkok for giving me a chance to learn to cook! The first cooking classes I taught were at Jasmine Market Grocery, so I would like to thank those students who took classes from me and who encouraged me to write a cookbook. A big thank you to the many school districts around the Twin Cities that gave me an opportunity to teach Thai cooking classes through Community Education -- I'm very grateful!

I would especially like to thank all of the Community Education students who have taken cooking classes from me and who encouraged me to write a cookbook -- thank you for your support!

A big thank you to my in-laws, Bob and Jean, for their encouragement and support, and Happy 50th Anniversary. Many thanks to Neil Ross for his assistance in the making of this cookbook. Thanks to Carl Oppedahl for all of his assistance and support. Thanks to all of my friends in the Thai Association of Minnesota. Thanks to my brothers and sisters and all their children for their help, encouragement and love!

And finally, a big thank you to my husband Randy and son Tom. I couldn't have done it without you, thanks for everything!

This book is dedicated to my dad,
Don Khommuangpak.

Table of Contents

Preface..1

Introduction..3

A Little Bit About Northeast Thailand (Isaan)..................................6

Ingredients & Equipment Used in Thai Cooking

Fresh, frozen, and dried ingredients...18
Noodles (fresh and dried)...38
Canned, bottled, and packaged ingredients....................................40
Cooking equipment..45

Some Thoughts on Thai Cooking..49

Crying Tiger Recipes: Appetizers

Egg Rolls with Pork (Paw Piah Tod)..52
Sweet & Sour Sauce for Egg Roll..53
Thai Spring Rolls (Paw Piah Soad)...54
Sauce for Spring Roll..55
Pork Satay with Peanut Curry Sauce..56
Ar Jard Sauce...57
Tapioca Dumpling with Pork (Sakoo Sai Moo).............................58
Mieng Kham & Sauce..60
Thai Lettuce Wraps (Pae Za Pun)...62
Tamarind Peanut Sauce for Lettuce Wraps.....................................63
Shrimp on Lemon Grass Skewers (Goong Obe Ta-krai)..............64
Crispy Rice Noodle (Mee Grob)...66
Fried Wonton with Pork (Giow Grop Moo) & Dipping Sauce...............68
Son-in-Law Eggs (Kai Luke Koei)..70
Curry Puff..72
Crispy Sarong Appetizer..74
Thai Fish Cakes (Tod Mun Pla)..76

Fried Chicken Wings (Peek Gai Tod)..78
Stuffed Chicken Wings (Peek Gai Yod Sai)..79
Pork Toast (Kanom Punk Na Moo)...80
Crab Roll (Hoy Jaw)..81
Chicken in Pandan Leaves (Gai Hor Bai-toey).................................82

Crying Tiger Recipes: Salads

Green Papaya Salad (Som Tum Thai)..84
Isaan-Style Papaya Salad (Som Tum Pla Ra)....................................86
Isaan-Style Chicken Salad (Laab Gai)...88
Grilled Salmon Salad (Laab Pla Salmon)...90
Silver Bean Thread Noodle Salad (Yum Woon Sen).......................92
Pork Salad with Ginger (Nam Soad)...93
Squid Salad (Yum Pla Meuk)...94
Crispy Catfish with Green Mango (Yum Pla Duke Foo)................96
Lemon Grass Salad (Yum Ta-krai)..98
Waterfall -- Grilled Pork Salad (Plar Moo Nam Toke)...................99

Crying Tiger Recipes: Soups

Noodle Soup with Beef (Kuay-tiaw Nua).......................................100
Thai Hot and Sour Shrimp Soup (Tom Yum Goong)...................102
Chicken and Coconut Milk Soup (Tom Kha Gai)........................104
Clear Noodle Soup with Tofu (Gang Jeud Woon Sen).................106
Wonton Soup with Pork (Gio Nam Moo)......................................107
Sour Curry Soup with Shrimp (Gang Som Goong)......................108
Sour Curry Paste (Krueng Gang Som)..109
Pumpkin Coconut Soup (Fak Tong Gang Ka Ti)..........................110
Rice Soup with Pork (Kao Tom Moo)...111
Chicken Bone Soup Broth..112
Beef Bone Soup Broth, Pork Bone Soup Broth.............................113

A Little Bit About Rice..114

Crying Tiger Recipes: Rice Dishes

Jasmine Rice (Kao Homm Mali) & Sticky Rice (Kao Niaw)..................116
Fried Rice with Pork (Kao Pad Moo)..................117
Pineapple Fried Rice with Shrimp..................118
Yellow Curry Fried Rice with Shrimp (Kao Pad Pong Karee)..................120
Chicken and Rice with Ginger Sauce (Kao Mun Gai)..................122
Fried Rice Cake with Red Curry (Kao Tod Nam Kluke)..................124

Crying Tiger Recipes: Thai Stir-fries

Stir-fried Beef with Holy Basil (Nua Pad Bai Grapow)..................126
Stir-fried Sweet and Sour Pork (Moo Pad Prio Wan)..................128
Stir-fried Pork with Ginger (Moo Pad King)..................130
Stir-fried Pork with Thai Basil (Moo Pad Horapha)..................131
Stir-fried Pork with Peanut Curry Sauce (Pra Rahm Long Song)..................132
Stir-fried Chicken with Cashew (Gai Pad Med Ma Muang)..................134
Stir-fried Chicken with Peapods (Gai Pad Tua-luntow)..................135
Chicken with Lemon Grass (Gai Tod Ta-krai)..................136
Catfish with Holy Basil (Pla Duke Pad Phet Bai Grapow)..................138
Scallops in Choo Chee Sauce (Choo Chee Hoy Shell)..................140
Squid with Green Peppercorns (Pla Meuk Pad Prik Thai On)..................141
Stir-fried Prik King Curry with Seafood (Prik King Pad Talay)..................142
Cha-om Omelette (Kai Tod Cha-om)..................144
Shrimp Paste Dipping Sauce (Nam Prik Kapi)..................145
Water Spinach with Soyabean Sauce (Pak Boong Fie Dang)..................146
Chive Flowers with Tofu..................148

Crying Tiger Recipes: Noodle Dishes

Drunken Noodle with Chicken (Kuay-tiaw Pad Kee Mao)..................149
Pad Thai with Chicken..................150
Isaan-Style Noodles with Pork (Pad Mee Isaan)..................152
Silver Bean Thread Noodle with Seafood (Pad Woon Sen Talay)..................154

Wide Rice Noodle with Beef (Rad Na Nua)...156
Rice Noodle with Black Soy (Pad See-iew)...158
Rice Noodle with Catfish Curry (Kanom Jeen Numya Pla)...................160

Crying Tiger Recipes: Thai Curries

Green Curry with Pork (Gang Kiowan Moo)..162
Green Curry Paste (Krueng Gang Kiowan)..163
Red Curry with Chicken (Gang Dang Gai)...164
Red Curry Paste (Krueng Gang Dang)..165
Massamun Curry with Beef (Gang Massamun Nua)................................166
Massamun Curry Paste (Krueng Gang Massamun)..................................167
Pork with Yellow Curry (Gang Karee Moo)...168
Yellow Curry Paste (Krueng Gang Karee)...169
Isaan-style Beef Curry (Om Nua)...170
Isaan-style Bamboo Shoot Soup (Gang Naw Mai)....................................172
Bitter Melon with Catfish (Gang Om Mara Pla Duke)...........................174

Crying Tiger Recipes: Fish & Seafood

Steamed Rainbow Trout with Young Ginger..176
Steamed Seafood in Red Curry (Hor Moke Talay)....................................178
Steamed Walleye with Vegetables (Pla Noong Pak)..................................180
Young Green Pepper Sauce (Nam Prik Noom)..181
Grilled Scallops in Banana Leaves (Ab Hoy Shell)...................................182
Grilled Tilapia in Pandan Leaves (Pla Nin Pun Bai-toey)......................183

Crying Tiger Recipes: Pan-fried & Grilled Meats

Garlic and Pepper Pork (Moo Tod Kra-tiem Prik-tai)............................184
Grilled Chicken (Gai Yang)..186
Crying Tiger (Sua Rong Hai)...188

Crying Tiger Recipes: Thai Desserts

Mango with Sticky Rice (Kao Niaw Ma Muang).....................................190
Tapioca Combo Dessert (Ruam Mit)...191

Yellow Mung Bean Dessert (Dao Suwan)..192
Banana in Coconut Milk (Kluay Buat Chee)..193
Agar-agar with Coconut Cream (Woon Ka Ti)...194
Black Sticky Rice Dessert (Kao Niaw Dum Peiuk)..................................195
Grilled Yucca with Coconut Cream (Mun Sum Pa Lung Ping).............196
Sweet Yucca with Coconut Cream (Cherm Mun Sum Pa Lung)...........198
Baked Thai Custard (Kanom Mor Gang)..199
Boniato Ball Dessert (Kanom Kai Noke Gratah).....................................200

Crying Tiger Recipes: Thai Cooking for Kids

Tommy's Scrambled Eggs with Green Onion...202
Thai French Fries, Onion Rings, and Hot Dogs......................................203
Baked Chicken Drummettes (Gai Ope)...203
Stir-fried Pork with Oyster Sauce and Tofu..204
Thai Beef Jerky (Nua Tod)...204
Beef and Potato with Oyster Sauce...205
Sticky Rice Dumplings..205
Thai Chow Mein (Goy See Mee)...206
Fried Catfish (Pla Duke Tod Grob)..206
Thai-style Udon Noodle Soup (Kao Pearng Sen)....................................207
Veggie Combo (Pad Pak Roum)...207
Condominium (Multi-layered Dessert)..208
Thai Shaved Ice..208
Thai Pancake (Kanom Kroke)...209
Floating Balloons Dessert (Bua Loy)...209

Sources for Thai Ingredients Online..210

Index..211

Preface

I moved from Thailand to America about 15 years ago. In an effort to let my new family and friends learn a little bit about Thailand, I began cooking Thai food for them (this was before there were lots of Thai restaurants in the Twin Cities). They enjoyed the food and many of them asked if I could write down some of the recipes for them. Later, when I began teaching Thai cooking classes, many of my students encouraged me to write a Thai cookbook.

The title of this book, "Crying Tiger", is taken from the Thai dish of the same name, which originated in Northeast Thailand. Featuring beef marinated in spices and grilled over charcoal, Crying Tiger gets its name from both the stripes on the meat created by the grill and the juices dripping off of the meat (which resemble tears). Thai people really enjoy giving interesting and playful names to food and some other examples include: Waterfall (Grilled Beef Salad); Drunken Noodles; Dancing Shrimp; Volcano Chicken (a roasted chicken with whisky sprinkled on top is lit before serving so it looks like a volcano); Thunderstorm (the name refers to the sound roasted tamarind seeds make in your mouth); Condominium (a multi-layered dessert that resembles a condo); Heaven and Hell Dipping Sauces (Heaven is a mild, sweet sauce while Hell is extremely spicy); and Son-in-Law Eggs. Food is taken very seriously in Thailand, but people like to have fun with it too!

My goal in writing this book was to share some of my favorite Thai recipes, but also to share a little bit of information about Thai culture and customs. The subtitle of the book, "Thai Recipes from the Heart", refers to the fact that many of the recipes in this book were handed down from my family and were never written down until now. As in any culture, food is an important way of passing down history to the next generation.

Over 100 Thai Recipes are included in the book, with an emphasis on the foods of Northeast Thailand, the place of my birth. In addition to the recipes, a section of the book is devoted to many of the ingredients and equipment used in Thai cooking. Finally, there's a section at the end of the book devoted to Thai cooking for kids, which my son thought was a good idea because he's been cooking Thai since he was about 7 years old!

Introduction

Boom, boom, boom!

Thwack, thwack, thwack!

Pound, pound, pound!

These sounds were heard everyday in my house growing up and though they sounded like construction noise, they were actually the sounds of my mom pounding out Som Tum (Green Papaya Salad) in her kloke, which is the same as a mortar and pestle. A kloke can be found in most homes in Isaan (or Northeast Thailand) where I grew up, and they're used to make Som Tum, Tum Tang (Cucumber Salad), Tum Ma Muang (Mango Salad), and dipping sauces called Nam Prik. Entire meals can be constructed using only a kloke and fresh vegetables, herbs, and spices.

Growing up I was expected to help out around the house before and after school. I would clean the house, wash clothes, get groceries, and whatever else my mom needed help with. She was born and raised in Udon Thani, a city in Northeast Thailand, and she would primarily make Isaan food. One of the signature ingredients is pla ra, or fermented fish sauce, which differs quite markedly from the bottles of clear fish sauce sold in Asian markets. Traditionally, it's made in the home from fish, water, salt, and roasted rice powder, and it has a very pungent aroma; some would even go so far as to say it stinks. My mom would make her version of pla ra, put it in a jar, and leave it for at least a year, but the longer the better. Her food was renowned in our neighborhood for being extremely spicy, especially her Som Tum, which was so spicy you could hardly breathe while eating it!

My dad, also from Isaan, was born and raised in Korat, which is much closer to Bangkok than Udon Thani. Because of that, he was familiar with many different types of food. In his travels throughout Thailand he sampled food from India, Burma, Malaysia, Vietnam, Japan, and even the West. He loved to try new things and he wanted to learn how to make them himself.

When I was a teenager, a relative of ours came to my dad and asked if he would allow me to go with him to Bangkok to help out with his restaurant. I was very interested in this because I had never been to the big city and I wanted to see what it was like. My mom was dead-set against it and thought it would not be a good idea for a teenage girl to be living in the big city so far away from her parents. My dad was more open to it and thought I could handle being so far away from home. So I moved to Bangkok and began working at a very popular restaurant called Porn Isaan, which in Thai means "best wishes from Isaan".

My duties at the restaurant included waitressing, bussing dishes, food prep, and anything else that needed to be done. We would work long shifts and we got to eat the same food that the customers ate. There was one dish in particular, Pla Duke Pad Phet, or Catfish Curry, that I really liked. Normally during break times, my co-workers would sleep or perhaps eat or go shopping, but I decided that I was going to find out how the chef made the Catfish Curry. So, on my breaks, I began to hang around the kitchen, peeking around corners to try and learn the ingredients of the dish and how it was prepared. The chef did not want any waiters or waitresses looking over his shoulder while he was cooking, so he would shoo me out of the kitchen. That didn't stop me, and though my friends laughed at me for wasting valuable sleeping time hanging around the kitchen, I did manage to get what I thought was the recipe for the Catfish Curry.

Every few months or so, we would get a few days break to go home and visit our families. On my first trip home, I decided I would make the Catfish Curry for my dad. I gathered together all of the ingredients and prepared the dish as best I could remember from looking over the chefs' shoulder. My dad tasted it and said it was very delicious (aroy dee in Thai), but he added that it was missing something. Now I was bound and determined to go back to Bangkok and find out what that missing ingredient was.

Back at work, I redoubled my efforts to peek over the chefs' shoulder and one day I finally learned what the missing ingredient in the recipe was -- half and half! We call it cream in Thailand, but it's basically just half and half. So now, despite being made fun of by my co-workers, I had all the ingredients for the Catfish Curry. My next trip home I made the dish again for my dad and this time he said it was perfect -- aroy dee tee sute! (the most delicious in Thai). I was so proud of myself and that was really the beginning of my desire to learn everything about Thai cooking. The saying "the way to someones' heart is through their stomach" is doubly true in Thailand.

I ended up working at the restaurant for several more years and I gained a lot of experience learning to cook and serve Thai food. I also became great friends with the chef and my experience at the restaurant, along with everything I learned from my mom and dad, was the foundation for my love of cooking. It's my hope that the recipes in this book will help you learn to prepare delicious Thai food for your family, friends, and loved ones!

The author (front row, second from left) at Porn Isaan Restaurant

A Little Bit About Northeast Thailand (Isaan)

Northeast Thailand and Isaan are used interchangeably in this book. Northeast Thailand, of course, refers to a geographic location in Thailand and Isaan (pronounced e-saan) usually refers to the people, culture, and food of that region, though they are truly interchangeable. Stretching from Nakhon Ratchasima (Korat) in the south to Nong Khai in the north and Ubon Ratchatani in the east, Northeast Thailand differs greatly from the other regions in Thailand. Except during the rainy season, the climate in Isaan is very dry -- even drought-like. Before much of the land was cleared for logging and agriculture, it was a very lush, green forested region.

The Mekong River makes up much of the northern and eastern border of Isaan, and in the past the river provided much of the fish eaten in the region. Giant catfish, some over 15 feet in length, were once very common in the Mekong, however overfishing has caused their numbers to dwindle considerably.

The cuisine of Northeast Thailand differs quite a bit from the other regions of the country. Sticky rice (kao niaw in Thai) and Isaan people go hand in hand, indeed sticky rice is often eaten by hand -- it's rolled into a little ball and used to grab bits of vegetables, meat, and sauces. Along with sticky rice, Isaan is famous for Som Tum, Gai Yang (barbecued chicken), Laab (meat salad), and Nam Toke (Waterfall grilled beef salad). Other notable dishes include Hor Moke, Om, and Gang Naw Mai. Vegetables such as pac peow, kayang, kowtong, saw leaf herb, and many others are eaten with most meals. Pla ra fish sauce holds a special place in Isaan cuisine, the aromatic liquid is used not only in Isaan-style Som Tum, but in various types of Nam Prik dipping sauces.

A favorite way to eat sticky rice in Isaan is to barbecue it (shown right). Kao Gee consists of cooked sticky rice which is pressed together, placed on a bamboo skewer and brushed with salt and egg. It's then barbecued, often on a home-made grill constructed from half of an oil drum. This snack is typically available during the winter months and at festivals.

Kao Lam, a favorite dessert, is made from sticky rice, coconut milk, and black beans. They're combined in a hollowed-out piece of bamboo, then grilled over a charcoal fire, which adds a subtle, smoky flavor to the rice. After cooking, most of the bamboo is removed (shown left), leaving just a very thin layer of it, which both adds flavor and holds the Kao Lam together for eating.

Sticky rice is also known as glutinous rice, and that explains one of the main reasons it has been eaten in Isaan for many, many years. For farmers, construction workers, and others laboring in extreme heat, there was a need for food which would provide long-lasting energy -- something that would stick to the ribs. Aside from the nutritional boost from sticky rice, it is of course eaten by hand so it doesn't require any utensils. Isaan people in general tend to enjoy spicier food than that in other regions of Thailand, so that's yet another reason for eating sticky rice -- it helps to protect the stomach from hot chilies. In addition to enjoying spicy foods, many in Isaan love to eat very sour or very bitter foods. It's not uncommon to be served a variety of pickled vegetables at meals, including mustard greens, yu choy, cabbage, green onions, pak sadao, bitter melon, and eggplant.

Northeast Thailand is not generally at the top of the list of tourist destinations in Thailand, but journeying to Isaan offers an opportunity to see a traditional way-of-life that is fast disappearing in much of the country. In addition, there are many customs that are unique to the region. In Isaan, it's very common to rise early and prepare food, a portion of which is given to monks who walk through the community at daybreak (shown above). People place food into their bowls as they pass by; in fact, the monks are only supposed to eat food which is given to them as alms by area residents.

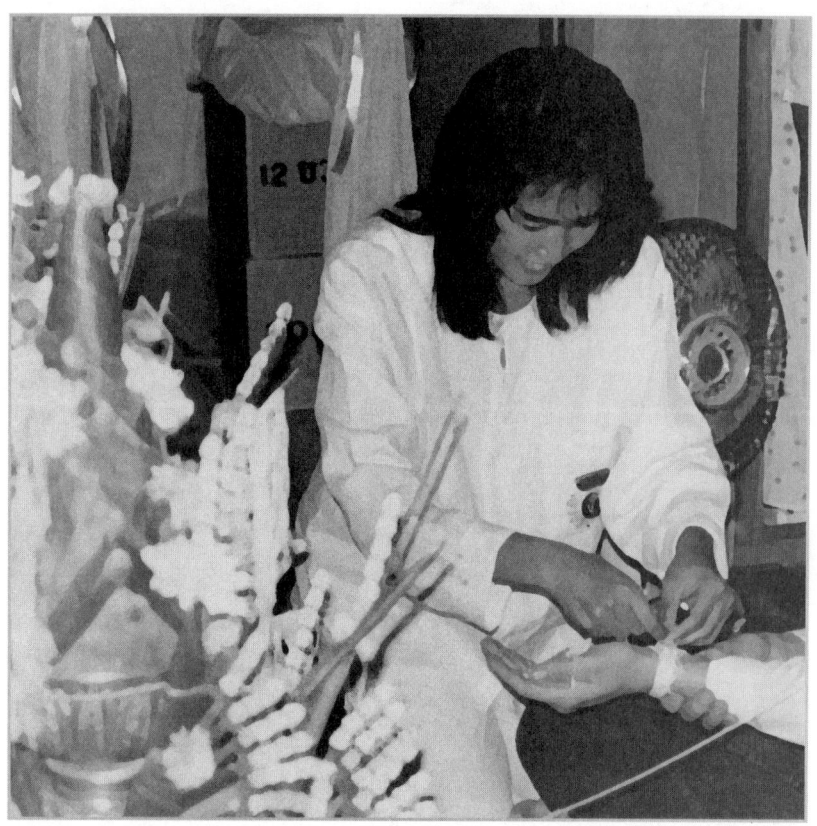

As a gesture of good luck, it's very common in Isaan to tie a string around the wrist of someone who's getting married (shown above). The ceremony is also done for a mom and her new baby, to welcome family and friends arriving for a visit, or to wish good luck to those departing on a trip.

Strings are also tied around the wrists of those who are sick to wish them a speedy recovery. The ceremony, which is called su-kwan, is considered a way to pay respect and offer wishes of good luck to the person around whose wrist the string is being tied. The Thai phrase for wishing good luck is "choke dee" and it's spoken by the person tying the string. It's not uncommon in Isaan to see someone with hundreds of pieces of string around their wrist -- that's a lot of choke dee!

Wedding ceremonies in Isaan feature two objects which bear a resemblance to a Christmas tree (shown right), though they're constructed primarily from banana leaves. Known as pa-kwan, there's one for the bride and one for the groom. Festooned on the pa-kwan are garlands of fresh flowers, known as doke rawk (flowers of love), as well as candles and money (the currency is intended to provide a good financial start for the couple). Strings run from the pa-kwan to both the bride and groom, through which good luck and best wishes for their future are supposed to be carried. The parents of the bride and groom tie strings around their wrists, followed by relatives and friends.

Traditionally in Isaan, meals are eaten while seated on the floor, often on a bamboo mat (shown left). The various dishes are placed in the center and are eaten family-style. The women are customarily seated with their legs to one side, while the men sit cross-legged. This is a custom which has been followed in Isaan for perhaps hundreds of years.

A Little Bit About Northeast Thailand (Isaan)

A favorite dish at picnics is fish grilled on a bamboo skewer over charcoal (shown above). But perhaps the most famous picnic dish is dancing shrimp, so-called because they're still alive when they're eaten. Hot chilies and other spices are added to the shrimp and they do indeed dance around the mouth on their way down! The Thai word for fun is sanook and waterfalls are very sanook! They're a favorite place for picnics, and the one shown below, called Than Tong, cascades down into the Mekong River. It's a great way to cool off during a hot day.

One of the most common reasons for visiting Isaan is because it's a major gateway to Laos, particularly by way of the Friendship Bridge, which spans the Mekong River at Nong Khai (shown above). A major tourist attraction in Nong Khai is Sala Gaew Goo, also called Wat Khaek (shown below), which features many large cement statues.

Fairs are held throughout Isaan which are very similar to state or county fairs in America. Many types of food are available, as well as traditional arts and crafts. In the photo above, singers are enticing customers to watch motorcyclists ride around the inside of a barrel at high speeds. Amusement rides, such as the ferris wheel (shown below), are favorite attractions and vendors sell clothing, furniture, music cd's, vcd's, and just about anything else imaginable. Fairs are a wonderful way to experience life in Isaan.

Visitors to Isaan during the rainy season, which runs approximately from July to September, may very likely see newly-planted rice fields (shown above). Numerous varieties of vegetables and fruits are grown year-round, including a very important tree to Isaan people -- the papaya tree! The papayas shown at right are green and ready to be picked and made into Som Tum. Papaya, which in Thai is called malagaw, grows everywhere in Thailand, but nowhere is the unripe fruit more highly prized than in the Northeast.

A unique mode of transport called a saamlor (shown above) can still be found in many cities in Isaan. It's a human-powered people delivery system that requires only human energy, no fossil fuels. Known elsewhere in Asia as pedicabs, they can be found in Udon Thani and other cities in Isaan. The hot dog man (shown below) is a common site in the Northeast, and other merchants peddle (sometimes literally pedaling) their goods to customers all over the countryside. In fact, there are trucks that contain virtually an entire grocery store that supply those who live far from town. And of course there are ice cream and shaved ice vendors, as well.

Visitors to Isaan will undoubtedly hear two unique forms of music while in the region, morlam and luke toong. Whether blaring from a radio in a cab (also true in Bangkok, as most of the cab drivers are from Isaan!), or coming from a restaurant, home, or store, music is very important to Isaan culture. Many families have VCD players that play karaoke disks, which allow family members to sing along with the music, while watching videos of their favorite artists singing.

Morlam is a very old, traditional type of music that features strong rhythms and an unusual type of singing. A morlam song will often have an opening section that's slower than the rest of the song, which then gives way to faster singing that occasionally sounds like the rap music of today. Singers are often accompanied by musicians playing the kaen (shown right), an instrument that's constructed from bamboo reeds. The kaen player blows into the instrument and a sound is produced that's a cross between a harmonica and an accordion. Holes in the reeds are covered and un-covered by the fingers, creating different tones. Nowadays, electric instruments also accompany the singers, but in the past it was strictly acoustic. Often when someone dies in Isaan, a morlam concert is held at the home of the deceased, and all the relatives, friends, and neighbors gather to remember the loved ones' life. Morlam music is one way in which Isaan culture is handed down from one generation to the next.

Luke toong, also known as country music, is the more modern of the two types of music. Borrowing elements from both pop and rock music, luke toong songs often tell the story of a boyfriend (or girlfriend) who leaves Isaan to go to Bangkok to make money for the family. Much of the subject matter is in fact similar to that in American country music, with an emphasis on broken hearts and broken dreams. The most famous luke toong singer, and the one who really popularized the music, was Pumpuang Duangchan, who unfortunately died in 1992 at the age of only 31. Her extraordinary vocal skills and ability to convey the emotion of the lyrics made her a beloved figure in Thailand. Her recordings are still very popular in Isaan (and the rest of Thailand).

For those thinking of visiting Thailand, a trip to Isaan is highly recommended. The people of Isaan are generally pretty friendly, and of course the food alone is worth the trip!

A woman fishes near a temple on the road from Udon Thani to Ban Chiang in Isaan

Thai Ingredients & Equipment

Thai basil

Thai Basil (bai horapha in Thai) An essential ingredient in many curries and stir-fries, Thai basil has an anise-like flavor, and the stems and leaves have a purplish tint. Thai basil is also served with Noodle Soup (Kuay-tiaw) and is eaten raw as a vegetable. The leaves don't last very long and do not dry or freeze well, so they should be eaten as soon as possible.

holy basil

Holy Basil (bai grapow in Thai) Peppery is perhaps the best way to describe the taste of holy basil. Used primarily in stir-fries and soups, holy basil can be dried or frozen for later use, but fresh is best. There are two varieties, red or white, and the stems have hairs on them. Holy basil is not usually eaten raw, but it's sometimes deep-fried and eaten with Thousand Year Eggs (Khai Yeo Maa).

lemon basil

Lemon Basil (bai maengluck in Thai, e-too in Lao) Maengluck has a lemony, citrus-like flavor and is used primarily in soups like Pumpkin Coconut Soup and dishes such as Steamed Walleye. It's also eaten raw with Kanom Jeen Namya. It is possible to freeze or dry maengluck, but it's best to get it fresh and use it quickly as it doesn't keep long.

Lemon Grass (ta-krai in Thai)

Lemon grass, which is used in Thai soups, curries, and salads, is sold in many supermarkets now, as well as virtually all Asian markets. Featuring a subtle, lemony flavor, it's cut into pieces and used to flavor soups such as Tom Yum and Tom Kha Gai. Thin slices of the tender, middle part of the stalk are used in salads such as Yum Ta-krai. Frozen minced lemon grass is available at many Asian markets.

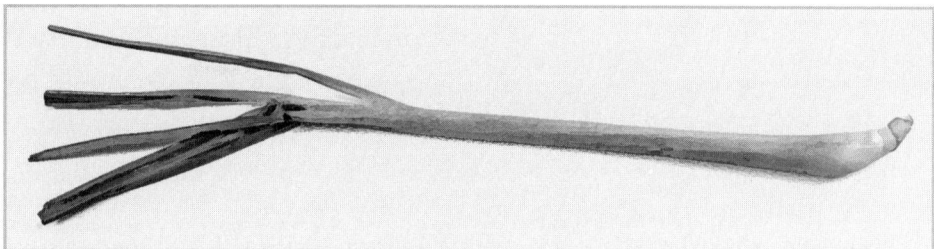

lemon grass

mint

Mint (salanae in Thai)

Peppermint is the variety of mint used most often in Thai cooking. Mint leaves are used in Spring Rolls and meat salads such as Laab and they're eaten fresh with Noodle Soup (Kuay-tiaw). Mint is sometimes available at supermarkets, but it's usually much cheaper to purchase it at Asian markets.

kaffir lime fruit and leaves

Kaffir Lime Leaves (bai makrut in Thai)

The aromatic leaves of the kaffir lime tree are used in many different Thai dishes. Whole lime leaves are used to flavor Tom Yum and Tom Kha soups. Minced lime leaves are used in Fish Cakes (Tod Mun Pla), meat salads, and curry pastes. Lime leaves are available fresh, frozen, or dried at most Asian markets.

cilantro

Cilantro (pak chee in Thai)
Cilantro, which is the leaf of the coriander plant, is used in many salads and soups, and is also eaten raw with meals. The root is used in some Thai dishes and the seeds are ingredients in several curry pastes and powders. Cilantro is available in most supermarkets and virtually every Asian market.

culantro

Culantro
(pak chee farang in Thai)
Also known as saw leaf herb (because the leaves have saw-like edges), culantro can be found in most Southeast Asian markets and has a taste somewhat similar to cilantro. Culantro is sliced for use in meat salads or Tom Yum soup, and is also eaten raw with Nam Prik dipping sauces.

pac peow

Pac Peow
(bai prik mah in Thai)
Pac peow is an herb that's eaten raw with many different dishes, especially those from Northeast Thailand. It tastes sort of like a cross between cilantro and mint (it's called Vietnamese mint in some Asian markets). It does not dry or freeze well, so it should be purchased as fresh as possible and eaten quickly.

prik kee noo

Thai Chili (Prik Kee Noo)
Perhaps the most famous Thai pepper, prik kee noo chilies are small in size but pack a real punch! They're used in Som Tum, Nam Prik Kapi, curries, stir-fries, and many other dishes. Prik kee noo chilies can be preserved by freezing.

prik noom

Young Green Pepper (Prik Noom)
Young green pepper is the main ingredient in Nam Prik Noom, a dipping sauce that's eaten with fresh vegetables and sticky rice. They're also grilled and used in meat salads. Prik noom is a mild-tasting pepper that can also be used in Green Curry (Gang Kiowan).

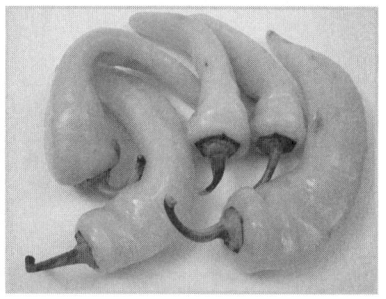
banana pepper

Banana Pepper (Prik You-awk)
This pale yellow pepper is very mild and is used in many stir-fries and dipping sauces. It can also be grilled and shredded for use in Beef Salad (Yum Nua Prik Pow). Banana peppers are available at most supermarkets.

dried red chili

Dried Red Thai Chili (Prik Kee Noo Hang)
Dried red Thai chili is ground for use in Green Papaya Salad (Som Tum), Meat Salad (Laab), Pad Thai, and many different curries. Whole dried chilies are roasted and eaten with Fried Rice Cakes (Nam Kluke) and other rice dishes.

chili pop

Chili Pop (Prik Yai Hang)
Chili pop, a dried pepper that's dark purple in color and 3-6 inches in length, is very mild and is used in Kanom Jeen Namya (primarily for coloring). It's available in most supermarkets as it's also used in Mexican cooking.

Thai Ingredients

long beans

Long Beans
(tua fak yaow in Thai)

Long beans, or yard long beans as they're sometimes known, are generally at least 12 inches in length and are much crunchier than regular green beans. They maintain their texture when cooked and are used in Som Tum, Prik King Curry, and many different stir-fries. Long beans are also eaten raw with meat salads (Laab). Try to select long beans that are thin, firm, and fresh!

green papaya

Green Papaya
(malagaw in Thai)

The main ingredient in Som Tum, green papaya is picked when it's not yet ripe, so the flesh is still very crunchy. Try to select a papaya that is firm, long, and smooth-skinned, as it will be easier to shred (and will have less waste). Green papaya is also used in Hot and Sour soup (Gang Som Malagaw).

green mango

Green Mango
(ma muang dip in Thai)

Green, unripe mango is used primarily for salads like Yum Pla Duke Foo (Fried Catfish Salad), and is also eaten raw with dipping sauce. Like green papaya, the flesh is very crunchy. Green mango, as well as green papaya, is available at Asian markets, particularly those catering to Thai, Lao, Cambodian, or Vietnamese customers.

Thai eggplant

Thai Eggplant
(makeua prau in Thai)

There are many varieties of eggplants eaten in Thailand, but the variety that's typically available from Asian markets here is green and white in color and 1-2 inches in diameter. Thai eggplants are very crunchy and are used in curries such as Gang Kiowan, soups, and Nam Prik. Thai eggplant is also eaten raw.

cherry eggplant

Cherry Eggplant
(makeua puang in Thai)

These tiny little round eggplants, measuring about ½ inch in diameter, are very bitter! They're steamed and eaten with Nam Prik and curries. Cherry eggplant can sometimes be difficult to find in Asian markets.

chinese eggplant

Purple Eggplant
(makuea muang in Thai)

Also known as Chinese eggplant, purple eggplant is generally 4-8 inches in length by 1-2 inches in diameter. Used primarily in Thai cooking for stir-fries, purple eggplant is available at most Asian markets. It can also be steamed and eaten with Nam Prik dipping sauce.

Thai Ingredients 23

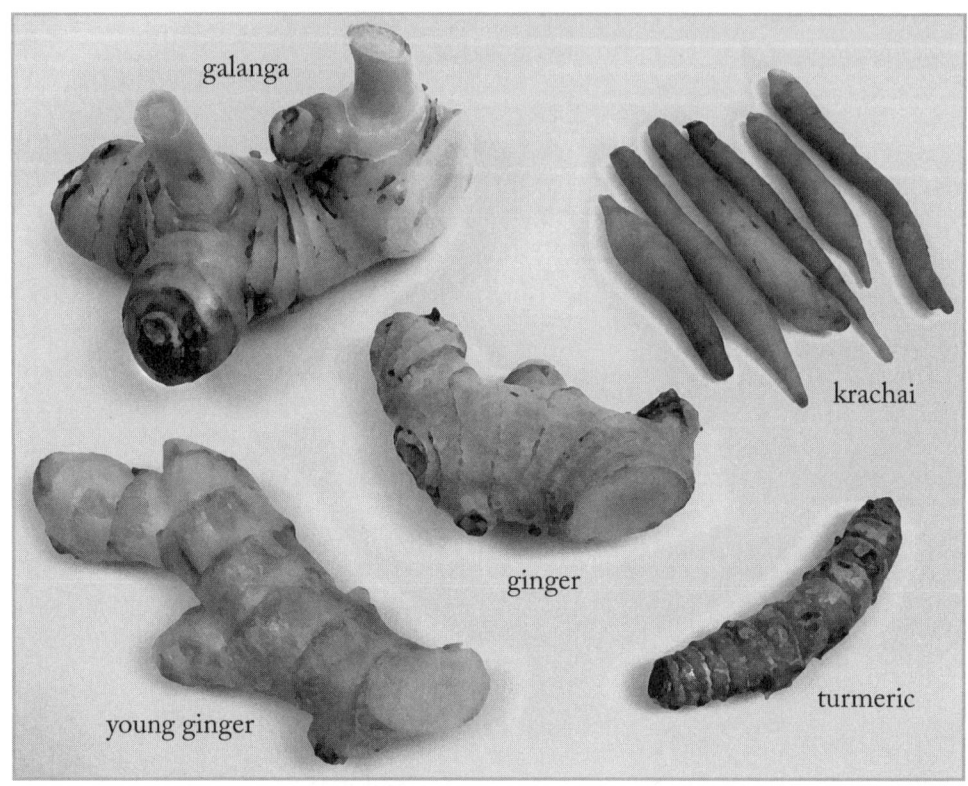

Ginger (king in Thai)
Ginger root is sliced or shredded for use in curries and stir-fries, diced for Mieng Kham appetizer, and used for flavoring drinks. Available in virtually all supermarkets, ginger can be frozen for later use.

Galanga (kha in Thai)
Galanga root is related to ginger, but has a smoother skin and a more subtle flavor. It's used in Chicken Coconut Soup (Tom Kha Gai), Sour Shrimp Soup (Tom Yum), as well as in some stir-fries and curries.

Young Ginger (king on in Thai)
Young ginger is picked earlier than ginger and has a yellowish, smooth skin. Used primarily in stir-fries, it can be more difficult to find than ginger.

Turmeric (ka-min in Thai)
A relative of the ginger family, turmeric is an ingredient in yellow curry powder and is also used to flavor and color food. Fresh turmeric can sometimes be found, but it's generally available either frozen or powdered.

Krachai (also called rhizome)
Sometimes called finger root (because the roots resemble fingers), krachai is also a relative of the ginger family. A key ingredient in Kanom Jeen Namya, krachai is generally not available fresh, only frozen or in jars.

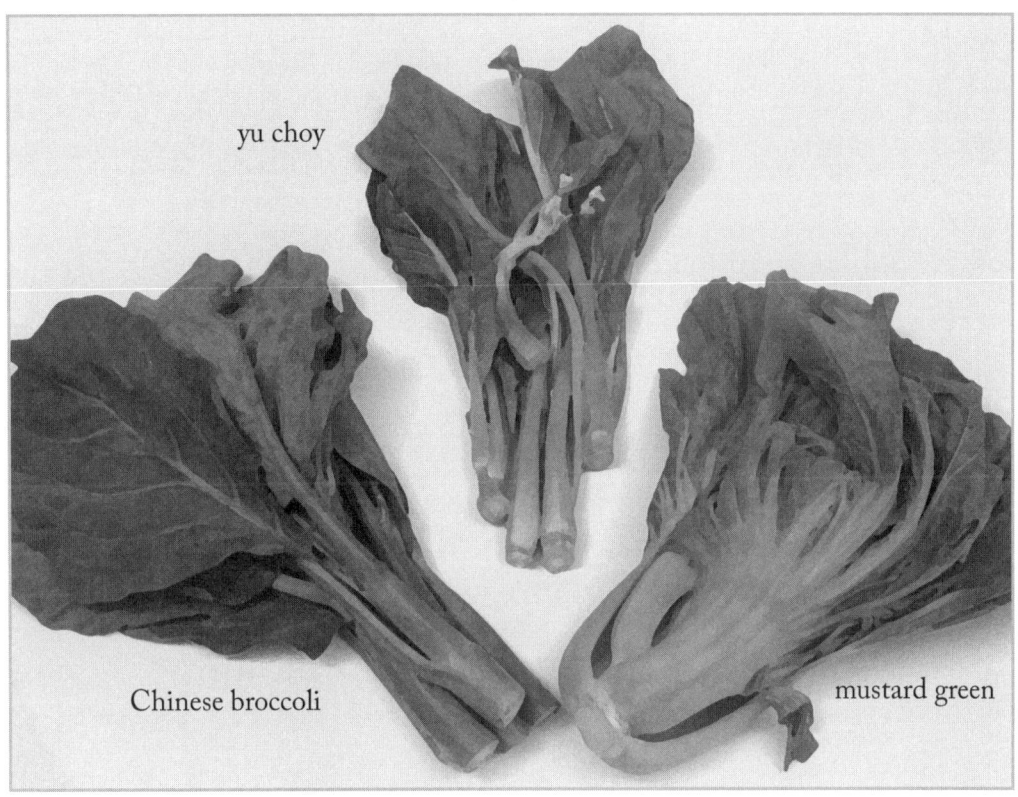

Chinese Broccoli (pak kana in Thai)
Chinese brocolli is often sold under its Cantonese name, gai-lan and it differs from regular broccoli both in taste and appearance. Gai-lan is milder-tasting and instead of florets (or flower heads), it has large green leaves. Used in many stir-fries and in noodle dishes such as Pad See-iew and Rad Na, Chinese brocolli (along with yu choy and mustard green), is available at most Asian markets and at many farmers' markets.

Yu Choy (pak gaat gwang toong in Thai)
Yu choy is often called Chinese flowering cabbage and one of the features of the vegetable are the small yellow flowers that grow on the stalks. It's used in stir-fries and soups, or is steamed and eaten with Nam Prik dipping sauces. When eaten raw, yu choy has a mustard-like flavor.

Mustard Green (pak gaat kiaw in Thai)
Also known as gai choy, mustard green is commonly made into pickles, which are eaten with Nam Prik dipping sauces. It's also used in soups such as Tom Jued Kraduke Moo.

fuzzy squash   smooth loofa gourd   opo squash

Fuzzy Squash (fak kiow in Thai)

Fuzzy squash (or hairy melon as it's also known), is used in both soups and stir-fries. The melon is typically 6-10 inches in length and the hairs must be removed before cooking. Fuzzy squash is sometimes called moqua in Asian markets. Fuzzy squash, along with loofa gourd and opo are often available at farmers' markets.

Smooth Loofa Gourd (buap hom in Thai)

There are two varieties of loofa gourd, smooth and ridged. Loofa sponges are made from the gourd, but it's also used in Thai cooking, mostly for soups and stir-fries. Loofa gourd is often called mawp in Asian markets.

Opo Squash (nam tao in Thai)

Opo, which is also known as bottle gourd or calabash, is a squash that's used in Thai soups and stir-fries. Pale green in color and about 6-12 inches in length, opo can be found in virtually all Asian markets and many supermarkets.

Coconuts used in Thai cooking

The juice of the young green coconut, (upper left, ma prow on in Thai) is a favorite drink in Thailand. The meat inside is eaten fresh or is used in desserts.

Shown at lower left is a young coconut (with the outer shell removed) as sold in Asian markets. The pointed tip of the coconut is cut open and a straw is inserted for drinking the fresh juice. The young coconut flesh is very delicious and can be scraped-off and eaten after the juice has been removed.

The medium coconut (shown upper right with the outer shell removed, ma prow tuen-turk in Thai) is picked between the young green coconut and the brown coconut. The shredded meat is most commonly used for desserts.

Coconut milk and coconut cream come from the brown coconut (lower right, ma prow gae in Thai). The flesh of this fully-mature coconut is scraped from the shell and squeezed to produce fresh coconut milk (ka ti in Thai).

bitter melon

Bitter Melon
(ma ra in Thai)

True to it's name, bitter melon is very bitter-tasting, though some of the bitterness dissipates during cooking. Only the outer skin of the bitter melon is used, the inside part containing the seeds is discarded. Pale green in color, bitter melon is generally 1-2 inches in diameter and 4-8 inches in length. It's used in stir-fries, soups, and teas and is also eaten steamed.

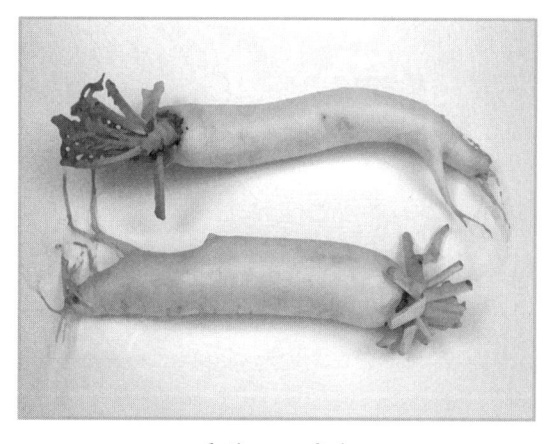

daikon radish

Daikon Radish
(hua pak gaat kao in Thai)

Daikon radish is primarily used in stir-fries and soups. Daikon is white in color, 1-4 inches in diameter and 5-15 inches in length. It has a very delicate flavor and a nice, firm texture. Preserved daikon is shredded and added to such dishes as Pad Thai and Sakoo Sai Moo.

green pumpkin

Green Pumpkin
(fak tong in Thai)

Green pumpkin, also called kabocha or Japanese pumpkin, is used in soups such as Pumpkin Coconut Soup. It's also steamed with fish and is used in many Thai desserts. Generally about 4-8 inches in diameter, green pumpkin is available in most Asian markets and many supermarkets.

shallot

Shallot
(homm dang in Thai)

Shallots, a member of the onion family, have a brownish-red paper skin and look somewhat like large garlic cloves. They have more flavor than regular onions and are commonly used in stir-fries, curries, soups, and salads.

Chinese celery

Chinese Celery
(kiern chai in Thai)

Though similar to regular celery, Chinese celery has stronger, more complex flavors. The stems are much thinner than regular celery and are hollow. Both the stem and leaves of Chinese celery are used in stir-fries, soups, and salads. Chinese celery is available in most Asian markets.

lotus root

Lotus Root & Rootlet
(hua bua in Thai)

Lotus root comes from the water lotus and is most often used to make desserts or drinks. A favorite dessert is simply lotus slices (with skin removed) boiled with water and sugar until the liquid turns to a syrup. Lotus root is also used in some stir-fries and soups.

dill

Dill (pak chee lao in Thai)
Dill is used a lot in Northeast Thai cooking, particularly in the steamed seafood dish featuring scallops called Ab Hoy Shell. Dill is also used in Beef Curry (Om) and is eaten raw as a vegetable. Though widely available in most supermarkets, dill is often much cheaper in Asian markets.

bean sprouts

Bean Sprouts (tua ngok in Thai)
Fresh bean sprouts are used in Noodle Soup (Kuay-tiaw), Pad Thai, Kanom Jeen Namya, and many other dishes. Sprouted from the seed of green mung beans, bean sprouts should be purchased as fresh as possible and used quickly, as they don't keep long. Canned bean sprouts should not be substituted for fresh.

bamboo shoots

Bamboo Shoots
(naw mai in Thai)
Bamboo shoots come in many different varieties and are eaten many different ways in Thailand. Shown at top are whole bamboo shoot tips which are used for Gang Naw Mai. Both bamboo strips (lower right) and shredded bamboo (lower left) are used in stir-fries and curries. They're available in Asian markets in either cans or jars.

Asian chives   chive flowers

Asian Chives & Chive Flowers
(gui chai & dok gui chai in Thai)
Asian chives are a member of the onion family and differ from regular chives in that the leaves are flat rather than round. With a light garlicky flavor, they're used in Pad Thai and other dishes. Chive flowers are the flowers of the Asian chive plant and are used in stir-fries and soups.

Edamame
Edamame are edible young soybean seeds and are most often steamed and eaten as a snack. They're available frozen in most supermarkets and can sometimes be purchased fresh at farmers' markets. Protein-packed, they make a very nutritious, delicious snack!

edamame

Pea Tips
(yot tua lan tao in Thai)
Pea tips are the tips of the peapod. With a taste that's crunchy and sweet (similar to peapods), pea tips are used in Gang Jeud soup. They're also used in stir-fries and are eaten raw with Nam Prik dipping sauces.

pea tips

Water Spinach
(pak boong in Thai)
Pak boong grows everywhere in Thailand and is very cheap to purchase. It's getting easier to find in America now, but it's often expensive and doesn't keep long. Usually grown in water, it's often sold under its Cantonese name, ong choy. Pak boong can be eaten raw or is cooked in dishes such as Pak Boong Fie Dang.

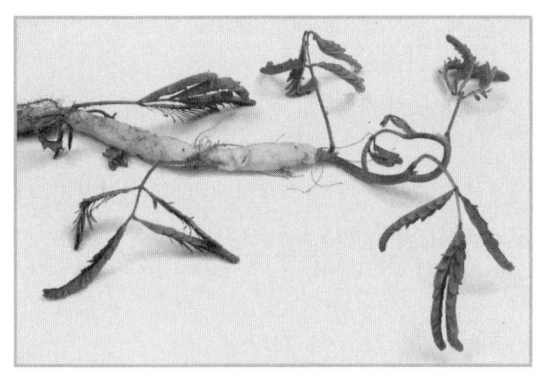

water spinach

Water Mimosa
(pak kra-chet narm in Thai)
Like pak boong, kra-chet grows in water and the white, foam-like material on the stem must be removed before cooking. Though similar in flavor to kra-tin, kra-chet has a more subtle taste. Kra-chet can be difficult to find in Asian markets.

water mimosa

Baby Bok Choy
(pak gaat shanghai in Thai)
Baby bok choy tastes the same as napa or regular bok choy. It's used in stir-fries and soups, and is steamed and eaten with Nam Prik dipping sauce. Baby bok choy is available at most Asian Markets and many supermarkets.

baby bok choy

kayang

lin fah

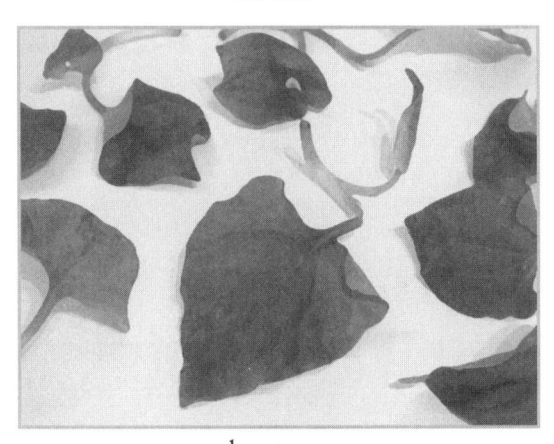

kowtong

bitter leaf

Kayang
Kayang is an herb that's used in Gang Naw Mai (bamboo tip soup), a Northeast Thai favorite. Kayang, which is also eaten raw, is best in bamboo shoot or fish dishes.

Lin Fah
Lin fah grows wild in Northeast Thailand, where it's eaten with Nam Prik dipping sauce. The flavor is a little bit bitter and a little bit sweet. Grilled lin fah is available frozen at some Asian markets. To serve, cut into slices and heat in a microwave.

Kowtong
Fishy and a little bit sour perhaps best describes the flavor of kowtong. It's eaten raw, especially in Northeast Thailand, with meat salads. Kowtong, as well as kayang and bitter leaf (cha-ploo), is available at Asian markets catering to Thai, Lao, Cambodian, or Vietnamese customers.

Bitter Leaf (bai cha-ploo)
In Thailand, cha-ploo is often eaten in place of lettuce leaves in the appetizer called Mieng Kham. Cha-ploo is also eaten with Coconut Gravy Noodles (Mee Ka Ti), and is used in a Northeast Thai curry called Om Hoy.

Thai Ingredients

wing bean

Wing bean
(tua poo in Thai)

Wing bean, which is very crunchy, is eaten raw and tastes somewhat similar to long beans. It's used in Hot and Sour Soup (Gang Som) or is thinly-sliced and used in place of long beans in Thai Fish Cakes (Tod Mun Pla).

sadao

Sadao

The leaves and flowers of the sadao plant are very bitter. They're eaten with Nam Prik with Grilled Catfish (Sadao Naum Pla Wan) or meat salads (Laab). Fresh sadao leaves are sometimes available at Asian markets, but the flowers are widely available frozen from Thailand.

cha-om

Cha-om

The leaves of the cha-om shrub have a most unique taste when eaten raw. Tod Kai Yod Cha-om features cha-om cooked in an egg omelette. Fresh cha-om is often quite expensive in an Asian market, but it's also available frozen from Thailand.

katin

Kra-tin

Kra-tin is eaten raw as a vegetable with Nam Prik and Som Tum and is somewhat similar in taste to cha-om. It comes in bunches of strings about 4-6 inches in length. Kra-tin, as well as wing bean, sadao, and cha-om, can be found in Asian markets catering to Thai, Lao, Cambodian, or Vietnamese customers.

tamarind

banana leaves

pandan leaves

Tamarind
(ma kham in Thai)

Tamarind is used many different ways in Thailand. It's eaten raw and is also an ingredient in candy. For cooking, it's available in concentrated form in slabs or in jars. The sour flavor of tamarind is featured in stir-fries, salads, soups, and curries. Refreshing juice drinks are also made from this versatile fruit.

Banana Leaves
(bai tong in Thai)

Banana leaves are available frozen in Asian markets and are used for wrapping up food prior to cooking. The flavor they impart during steaming could perhaps best be described as a very subtle, grassy flavor. The leaves are discarded after cooking.

Pandan Leaves
(bai toey in Thai)

Similar to banana leaves, pandan leaves are used for wrapping up food prior to cooking. The leaves impart a subtle flavor to the food that is somewhat similar to roasted young coconut juice. Fresh pandan leaves are not typically available, but frozen leaves from Thailand are generally pretty easy to find. An extract made from pandan leaves is used to flavor and color desserts.

Yucca Root
(mun sum pa lunk in Thai)
Primarily used in desserts, yucca root (also called cassava) is the source of tapioca. The taste of yucca, while similar to the potato, is much sweeter and richer. In Asian markets, this root is sometimes called yucca wax (the wax is applied as a preservative for shipping).

yucca root

Taro Root
(pueak in Thai)
Taro root is a tuber that tastes somewhat like the potato. There are several different varieties of taro and they're used most often in Thai cooking for desserts such as Baked Thai Custard (Kanom Mor Gang) or Taro in Coconut Milk. Taro root can be found in most Asian markets.

taro root

Boniato
(mun tet in Thai)
Boniato is similar to the sweet potato, only the flesh is white and the skin is purple. Boniato is used in Thai cooking to make desserts, especially deep-fried balls that resemble little donuts. It's also boiled or steamed and eaten plain. Boniato can be found in most Asian markets.

boniato

Jicama
(mun giew in Thai)

This sweet, crunchy tuber is shredded for use in salads and is also used in some stir-fries. Cooking does not reduce the crispiness of jicama, which can be found in most supermarkets.

jicama

Plantain Banana

Plantains, which look like green bananas, are also called cooking bananas, because they must be cooked before they can be eaten. They're usually boiled, steamed, or deep-fried. In Thailand, they're generally used in desserts or are eaten plain. Plantains are very easy to find in most supermarkets.

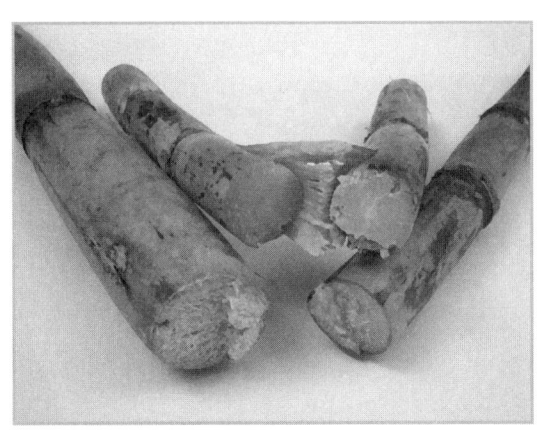

plantain

Sugar Cane
(oye in Thai)

It's very common to see kids in Thailand chewing on a piece of sugar cane for a snack, or drinking juice made from this versatile grass. Skewers made from sugar cane are often used for grilling shrimp over charcoal. Fresh sugar cane is available at some Asian markets and it's also available in either cans or jars.

sugar cane

Fresh Rice Stick Noodle

The preferred noodle for Noodle Soup (Kuay-tiaw), fresh rice stick is available at Asian markets and some supermarkets. Because the noodles are fresh, they need to be used fairly quickly or they'll start showing signs of mold (you can freeze the noodles, but they're best eaten fresh).

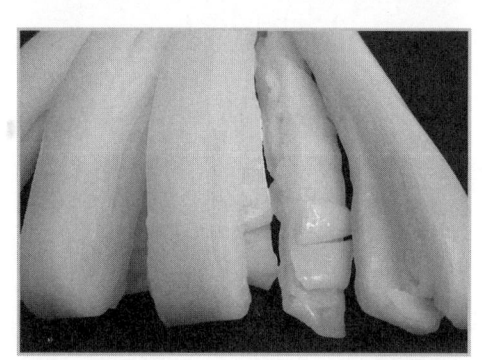

Fresh Wide Rice Noodle

Often called chow fun noodles, fresh wide rice noodles are used in dishes such as Rad Na and Pad See Mee. Sold in 1 or 2 pound packages, they're thin sheets of rice noodle available in either whole sheets or pre-cut into strips.

Dried Rice Stick Noodle

A dried version of fresh rice stick noodles, rice stick comes in a variety of widths, from small to extra large. Used in Noodle Soup and dishes such as Pad Thai and Drunken Noodle, rice stick is typically available in 1 pound packages.

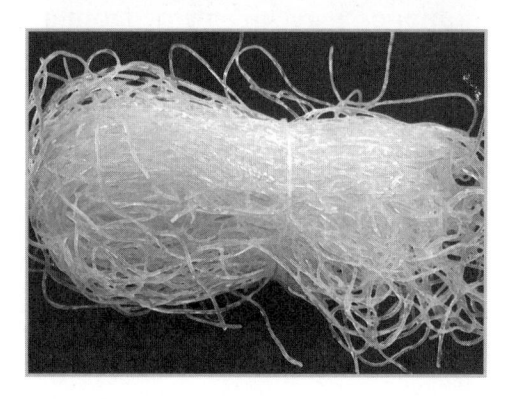

Dried Silver Bean Thread Noodle

Also known as cellophane or clear noodles, bean thread noodles are made from mung beans and are used in Egg Rolls, Pad Woon Sen, and Yum Woon Sen. Bean thread is sold in 1 or 2 pound packages, often wrapped with pink netting.

Dried Rice Vermicelli Noodle

Mee Grob, a Thai dish that features rice stick thrown into hot oil until it puffs up, is made from this variety of rice noodle. The noodles are available in 1 pound packages at most Asian markets.

Dried Thin Rice Noodle (Sen Mee)

Perhaps the thinnest rice stick available, this noodle is used to make the filling for Spring Rolls. Usually available in 8 ounce or 1 pound packages, sen mee can also be used to make dishes such as Noodle Soup or Rad Na.

Dried Imitation Egg Noodle

Salong, an appetizer that looks like little birds' nests, is made with imitation egg noodles. As the name implies, they contain no egg but resemble egg noodles. Available in Asian markets, they're most often sold in 1 pound packages.

Dried Guilin Rice Vermicelli

Guilin noodle gets it's name from a region in China and is used in the dish called Kanom Jeen Namya. They're also eaten as an accompaniment to Som Tum. Guilin rice noodles resemble regular spaghetti noodles and are typically sold in a variety of widths, most often in 1 pound packages.

Thai Ingredients

Fish Sauce (nam pla in Thai)

An essential ingredient in Thai cooking, fish sauce is a key source for the salty flavor in Thai food. Unlike salt, nam pla has deeper, richer flavors because it's fermented during production. In Thai cooking, fish sauce is usually not added until the very end, except when used in salads. Fish sauce is clear and amber-colored in appearance.

Fermented Fish Sauce (pla ra in Thai)

Pla ra is used often in Isaan cooking for main dishes, salads, soups, and Nam Prik sauces. Pla ra is brownish-grey in color, not clear, and pieces of fish are often visible in the liquid. Pla ra is considerably stronger smelling than regular fish sauce and is usually available in Southeast Asian markets.

Soy Sauce (see-iew in Thai)

The main ingredients in soy sauce are soybeans, wheat flour, salt, sugar, and water. It's used in stir-fries, marinades, and some dipping sauces.

Light Soy Sauce (see-iew kao in Thai)

Light (or thin) soy sauce is not just watered-down regular soy sauce; it's made to be lighter in flavor, but just as salty as regular soy sauce.

Black Soy Sauce (see-iew dum in Thai)

Black (or thick) soy sauce is much thicker than regular soy sauce and is used to color noodles in dishes such as Rad Na and Fried Rice. Molasses is added to thicken the sauce.

Mushroom Soy Sauce (see-iew hed homm in Thai)

Mushroom soy sauce is used in stir-fries and soups and is used in many vegetarian dishes. Healthy Boy is the preferred Thai brand.

Oyster Sauce (nam mun hoy in Thai)

Oyster sauce is used in stir-fries, soups, gravies, and to season meat and seafood. The preferred brand is Maekrua from Thailand (the label features a picture of a woman stir-frying).

Red, Green, Massamun, Karee, and Yellow Curry Pastes

In the past, curry pastes were typically made from scratch in a mortar and pestle. Pre-made curry pastes, found in most Asian markets, can be used for any of the curry recipes in this cookbook. Mae Ploy and Maesri are the recommended brands and come in either plastic tubs or small cans (any leftover curry paste can be frozen to preserve it).

Sriracha Chili Sauce (sauce prik in Thai)

Sriracha chili sauce, a bright orange-red dipping sauce used for seafood and meat, is also added as a condiment to Kuay-tiaw (Noodle Soup). Sriracha is a city located on the gulf of Thailand where the sauce originated.

Soyabean Sauce with Chili (nam prik pow in Thai)

This sweet and salty sauce contains sugar, shallot, soyabean oil, garlic, dried chili, fish sauce, dried shrimp, and tamarind paste. It has a very rich flavor that goes well with dishes such as Tom Yum, Fried Rice, and salads.

Yellow Soyabean Sauce (tow jiew in Thai)

Fermented whole soybeans are the main ingredient in tow jiew which is used in noodle dishes such as Rad Na, and to top steamed fish dishes. The yellow-colored sauce contains pieces of soybeans and should not be confused with regular soy sauce.

Shrimp Paste (kapi in Thai)

Made from small silver fermented shrimp, kapi is used in many dishes, particularly curries and Nam Prik dipping sauces. It's a very strong smelling essential Thai cooking ingredient.

Coconut Milk and Coconut Cream (ka ti and hoa ka ti in Thai)

A signature ingredient in Gang Dang, Gang Kiowan, and soups such as Tom Kha Gai, coconut milk is also used in many Thai desserts. Coconut cream is a thicker version of coconut milk. Both are available canned or frozen at Asian markets and many supermarkets.

Ground Thai Chili

Ground Thai chili is made from dried prik kee noo chilies. It's available either coarsely or finely ground in bags or plastic containers.

Sea Salt

Sea salt is recommended for use in this cookbook because the flavor is preferred over regular salt. Sea salt can be found in most Asian markets, as well as some supermarkets, and is available either coarsely or finely ground.

Madras Curry Powder

Madras curry powder, available at Asian or Indian markets, is used in Satay, Curry Puff, Curry-fried Rice, and Yellow Curry. Ingredients typically include curry, turmeric, chili, coriander, cumin seeds, cinnamon, cloves, bay leaves, allspice, and salt.

Palm Sugar & Coconut Sugar

Palm sugar (front row) and coconut sugar (back row) are sometimes referred-to as the same thing, though palm sugar comes from the toddy palm tree and coconut sugar comes from the coconut palm tree. Palm sugar, sometimes eaten as candy, is burned during cooking, so it has a smoky taste and a dark brown color. Coconut sugar is primarily used for cooking and is usually much lighter in color than palm sugar and milder tasting. Palm sugar (or coconut sugar) is available in Asian markets in small disks (sold in plastic bags), or in one big piece in a plastic jar. To make it easier to measure palm sugar, microwave in a bowl for 20-30 seconds and crumble the sugar into small pieces.

Egg Roll Wrappers

Sometimes confused with spring roll wrappers, egg roll wrappers are made from wheat flour and are sold in the frozen food section of Asian markets, typically in packages of 20, 25, 40, or 50 sheets. They're rolled up with noodles, veggies, and meat and deep-fried.

eggroll wrappers

Spring Roll Wrappers

Spring roll wrappers are made from rice and are used to make fresh spring rolls. Also called rice paper, they're thin, dried sheets typically sold in packages of 25 or 50 each. When purchasing rice paper, try to find sheets that are not broken into pieces.

spring roll wrappers

Rice Flour (pang kao jaow in Thai)

As the name implies, rice flour is made from rice and has many different uses in Thai cooking. Many desserts are made from rice flour and it's also used as a thickener. Unlike wheat flour, rice flour contains no gluten so it's safe to eat for those on gluten-free diets.

Glutinous Rice Flour (pang kao niaw in Thai)

Glutinous rice flour is made from sticky rice and is often used to make desserts, especially Bua Loy (which features balls made of sticky rice powder). Despite the name, glutinous rice flour does not contain gluten so it's safe to eat for those on gluten-free diets.

Tapioca Starch (pang mun in Thai)

Made from tapioca (which is processed from dried yucca root), tapioca starch is used to make the glue that holds egg rolls together prior to deep-frying. It's also an ingredient in desserts and is used to thicken stir-fries.

Roasted Rice Powder (kao kua in Thai)

Roasted rice powder is made from sticky rice which has been roasted and then ground into a powder. It's an essential ingredient in Isaan cooking and is available in Asian markets or it can be easily made at home. Simply roast uncooked sticky rice in a frying pan and then grind it into a powder.

Tamarind Concentrate (ma kham in Thai)

Tamarind concentrate is made from ripe tamarind fruit and gives a sour flavor to Gang Som (Hot & Sour soup), Pad Thai, and some dipping sauces. Tamarind concentrate is available in bottles or jars at most Asian markets.

Dried Shrimp (goong haeng in Thai)

Often used in Som Tum and Pad Thai, dried shrimp are simply baby shrimp which have been dried (usually in the sun). They are used whole or ground.

Star Anise & Cinnamon Stick

Star anise and cinnamon stick are dried ingredients used in making soup broth for Noodle Soup (see photo on page 112).

Agar-agar (woon in Thai)

Seaweed is the source of agar-agar, and that makes it a vegetarian version of jello. It's typically used in desserts and because it's transparent, ingredients can be suspended in it for a beautiful presentation. Agar-agar is available at Asian markets as a powder or in sticks, often colored with food coloring.

straw mushroom

oyster mushroom

wood ear mushroom

shiitake mushroom

puffball mushroom

Straw Mushroom (hed farng in Thai)
Featured in Tom Yum soup, straw mushrooms are available canned, either peeled (left) or unpeeled (right). Used in both soups and stir-fries, the unpeeled mushroom is much stronger-tasting than the peeled one.

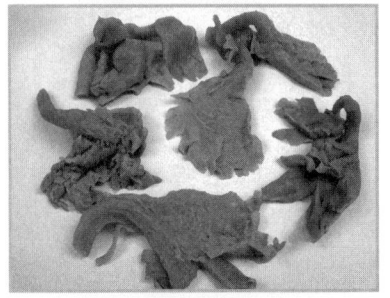

Oyster Mushroom (hed nang rom in Thai)
A main ingredient in Tom Kha Gai soup, oyster mushrooms are also used in stir-fries such as Bamboo Tip with Coconut Milk. Oyster mushrooms are available either fresh or canned.

Wood Ear Mushroom
(hed hoo noo in Thai)
Wood ears, also called black fungus mushrooms, are available dried, either whole or shredded. They're used in stir-fries, salads, soups, and stuffed chicken wings and must be soaked in water prior to use.

Shiitake Mushroom (hed homm in Thai)
Usually available in dried form, shiitake mushrooms must be soaked in warm water prior to use. They're featured in Stir-fried Pork with Ginger, Steamed Fish, and Fish Maw Soup.

Puffball Mushroom (hed pow in Thai)
Ranging in diameter from about ½ inch to 2 inches, puffball mushrooms are typically available in cans. They're used in soups such as Gang Naw Mai or are eaten as a side dish with dipping sauces.

Wok

The workhorse of the kitchen, woks come in different shapes, sizes, and in materials such as steel or aluminum (often with non-stick coatings). The bottom may either be rounded (it comes with a ring that holds it steady over the burner) or flat (so it can sit directly on the burner). If using a steel wok, it should be seasoned prior to use. Amazingly, woks used in restaurants may be as big as 2 or 3 feet across! The 12-inch frying pan (bottom) works great for making Pad Thai!

woks (and frying pan)

Mortar and Pestle (kloke in Thai)

Found in nearly every home in Thailand, the kloke is used to make Som Tum, Nam Prik, Curry Pastes, and many other dishes. Klokes can be made from clay, granite, or even wood and they're available from Asian markets in a variety of sizes.

mortar and pestle

Hot Pot

Used to keep soups hot during a meal, the hot pot has a slot at the bottom that holds a sterno pot. In Thailand, a meal may easily take 2 to 3 hours, so the hot pot is invaluable for keeping Tom Yum or Po-taek soups warm throughout the meal.

hot pot

Thai Cooking Equipment

3 tray steamer

bamboo steamer

bamboo steamer basket & aluminum pot

3 Tray Steamer

Made from aluminum, the 3 tray steamer is used in making such dishes as Steamed Fish, Hor Moke, and Saku Sai Moo. Water is brought to a boil in the bottom tray and food is placed on the upper trays for steaming. Because it does not breathe (like the bamboo steamer), food cooks faster in an aluminum steamer. Banana leaves, wax paper, or oil are often used to keep food from sticking to the trays during steaming.

Bamboo Steamer

Unlike aluminum steamers, a bamboo steamer is placed on top of a wok (or other pan) that has water boiling in it. It's often used to warm food since the top tray breathes. Both the bamboo steamer and the 3 tray aluminum steamer are available in various sizes at most Asian markets.

Bamboo Steamer Basket and Aluminum Pot

Used to make sticky rice (kao niaw), the steamer and pot combo is an essential tool in Northeast Thai cooking. Water is brought to a boil in the aluminum pot and the basket with the soaked sticky rice is placed on top of it (the basket can be used to drain the rice after soaking). A round pot cover is used to keep the steam from escaping.

Cooking Utensils

(chopsticks, spatula, chefs knife, carving knife, strainer, shredder, peeler)

Spatula Used along with a wok, a spatula is the main tool used in stir frying. Available in many sizes and lengths, the spatula pictured above is made from pounded steel and has a wooden handle on the end.

Chopsticks for cooking Long wooden chopsticks are invaluable when making noodle dishes such as Pad Thai and Drunken Noodles. They work much better than a spatula to separate the strands of noodles (to ensure that they all get flavored with the sauce).

Chefs knife and carving knife The chefs knife works great for dicing, mincing, slicing, and chopping. The carving knife is used for cutting meats and seafood. Also recommended is a Chinese cleaver, which works great for cutting and mincing meat (not shown).

Strainer Most often made of copper or steel wire, strainers are used primarily for deep-frying, though they can also be used for stir-frying. They're available at Asian markets in a variety of sizes and lengths.

Peeler and shredder A peeler is typically used for peeling the skin of green papaya, mango, carrot, or cucumber. The shredder is used to shred the flesh of papaya or mango into long, thin shreds.

Thai Cooking Equipment

Rice Cooker

Used in virtually every home in Thailand, a rice cooker is highly recommended. It not only makes cooking rice foolproof, but most models have a keep warm feature that keeps the rice warm for up to 12 hours. They typically come in 3 cup, 5 cup, or 10 cup sizes. Some restaurants use rice cookers that can cook up to 50 cups of rice at a time!

rice cooker

Clay Pots

Clay pots come in many different shapes and sizes. The clay pot at left is made for baking food in the oven. Shown at right is a combination clay pot with charcoal holder which can be used for either warming or cooking food. Both types of clay pots are available at most Asian markets.

clay pots

Sticky Rice Warmer

Made of handwoven bamboo, these baskets keep the rice warm and allow it to breathe during a meal (if you put it in a plastic container the rice will get too moist). Also, rice is never left uncovered during a meal. The baskets come in a variety of sizes and are available at most Southeast Asian markets. Some of the baskets are woven with different colors of bamboo, using different designs, and are quite decorative!

sticky rice warmer

Some Thoughts on Thai Cooking.....

Thai cooking is a balancing act, trying to find the right balance of sour, salty, spicy, and sweet flavors so that each dish turns out well. Because of this, you may want to think of the recipes in this book as starting points. If you follow them, you should end up with some very delicious meals. But to truly make them your own, you may wish to experiment a bit with amounts of ingredients, brands of ingredients, cooking times, and so forth.

The author teaches a cooking class

When I was growing up most curry pastes were made in a mortar and pestle; pre-made curry pastes existed, but they were not commonly used. I've included recipes for all of the curry pastes used in this cookbook, and if you're interested in making them, I encourage you to do so. However, I usually use the pre-made curry pastes and I recommend that you use them too. Similarly, when I was growing up, my mom made me crack open coconuts in order to scrape the meat from the shell (coconut milk is made from grated coconut meat). It's very hard work and now most people simply use canned coconut milk. The flavor is very good and it's a real timesaver!

Stir-frying, the most common cooking method used in Thai cooking, is often defined as cooking vegetables and meat in a wok over high heat with a small amount of oil while stirring constantly. In Thai cooking, a very hot wok is key and the vegetables and meat should be cut into small pieces ahead of time. Also, it's very helpful to pre-mix ingredients before adding them to the wok so they can go in at the same time. Cooking times can be very short and you don't want the vegetables or meat to get over-cooked! Finally, a good wok is highly recommended; it will make the job much easier!

Peanut oil is recommended for stir-frying and deep-frying, and vegetable oil will also work. Olive oil is not recommended for either stir-frying or deep-frying because the point at which it burns is much lower than that of either peanut oil or vegetable oil (though it works well in salads).

Virtually all of the ingredients and equipment used in this cookbook should be available at an Asian market near you. However, you may need to search out markets catering to Southeast Asian customers in order to find everything featured in this book. For a list of websites offering Thai ingredients for sale online, see page 210. For information about Thai cooking, recipes, preferred ingredients, cooking class information and more please visit my website, www.supatra.com.

Farmers' markets (shown left) are a great source for many of the fresh herbs, vegetables, and fruits used in Thai cooking and I highly recommend that you check them out. It's absolutely true that the fresher the ingredients, the better the dish will turn out! And quite often the produce is much cheaper than at a grocery store.

If you have a garden you can grow many of the ingredients used in Thai cooking. Websites offering seeds for many of the herbs, vegetables, and fruits used in Thai cooking include: www.evergreenseeds.com; www.johnnyseeds.com; www.newdimensionseed.com; www.agrohaitai.com; and www.green-seeds.com.

Some of the ways vegetables are cut in Thai cooking

sliced galanga

sliced yellow onion

stem-off lime leaf

diced shallot

chopped galanga

thinly-sliced lemon grass

thinly-sliced lime leaf

thinly-sliced shallot

Thai Recipes

Thai Egg Roll with Pork (Paw Piah Tod)

These deep-fried golden brown beauties are one of the most popular appetizers and are guaranteed to spice up any party!

1 pound ground pork (cook in boiling water for 5 minutes, drain, and set aside)
¼ pound dried silver bean thread noodle (soak in hot water until soft, drain, and cut in half)
5 cups shredded cabbage
½ cup shredded carrot
1 cup diced yellow onion
1 tablespoon minced garlic
½ cup chopped cilantro
½ teaspoon black pepper
½ tablespoon sugar
3 tablespoons oyster sauce
2 tablespoons light soy sauce
2 tablespoons soy sauce
½ teaspoon sea salt
4 tablespoons peanut oil
1 egg (beaten)
1 package frozen egg roll wrappers (20-50 sheets per package; defrost wrappers, carefully pull them apart and place in an airtight container)
1 tablespoon tapioca starch + ½ cup water (mix together, microwave for 1 minute and allow to cool; used to keep egg rolls from unrolling in hot oil)
oil for deep-frying

> **Tip for freezing Egg Rolls**
>
> To freeze Egg Rolls: deep-fry until lightly brown and allow to cool. Place in airtight plastic bag and freeze for up to 2 months.
>
> To reheat Egg Rolls: Preheat oven to 375 degrees. Place frozen Egg Rolls on a cookie sheet (do not defrost) and bake for 10 minutes. Microwaving is not recommended as the Egg Rolls become too soggy!

1. To make the filling, combine cooked ground pork, bean thread noodles, cabbage, carrot, onion, garlic, cilantro, black pepper, sugar, oyster sauce, light soy sauce, soy sauce, and salt in a bowl. Toss to mix but be careful not to mash the vegetables.

2. Heat a wok over high heat and add peanut oil, swirling to coat the entire surface. Add filling from step 1 and stir-fry for one minute. Make a place in the middle of the wok and add the egg, stirring constantly until scrambled. Mix scrambled egg with the filling and stir-fry for 5 minutes. Remove from heat and drain in a colander. Allow to cool before using.

3. Place an egg roll wrapper on a flat surface facing diagonally towards you and brush the far corner with a little tapioca glue. Place 2 tablespoons of

the filling approximately 3 inches in from the corner closest to you and fold the corner over the filling, then roll over several times. Fold both sides in towards the center and finish rolling up the wrapper. Preheat oil in a deep-fryer (or wok) to 375 degrees. Deep-fry the egg rolls for 3-5 minutes or until golden brown, then drain on paper towels. Serve with Sweet and Sour Sauce (see below).

Yield: 8 servings (makes approximately 25-30 egg rolls)

Sweet and Sour Sauce

½ cup sugar + 2 tablespoons
1 teaspoon sea salt
½ cup water

½ cup vinegar
⅓ cup ketchup
1 teaspoon sriracha chili sauce

Combine all of the ingredients in a saucepan and bring to a boil. Cook for 8 minutes, stirring occasionally, and remove from heat. Allow to cool before serving with Egg Rolls or any other deep-fried foods. Will keep for 1 month in the refrigerator.

Thai Egg Roll with Pork (Paw Piah Tod)

Fresh Spring Roll With Shrimp (Paw Piah Soad)

Summer is a wonderful time to make spring rolls because you can use whatever fresh vegetables are growing in your garden!

¼ pound dried rice noodles (thin vermicelli)
2 tablespoons peanut oil
1 clove garlic (minced)
3 tablespoons oyster sauce
1 tablespoon sugar
½ teaspoon black pepper
½ teaspoon sea salt
1 tablespoon hoisin sauce
1 teaspoon light soy sauce
½ cup chopped cilantro
⅓ cup mint leaves
⅓ cup shredded carrots
½ head iceberg lettuce (shredded)
1 pound medium-sized cooked shrimp
1 package rice paper (12 inch diameter)

> **Spring Roll Tip**
>
> Spring Rolls will keep in an airtight container for about 3-4 hours. After that the texture of the rice paper changes quite dramatically and the noodles and vegetables begin to dry out!

1. Fill a small soup pot with water and bring to a boil. Cook the rice noodles for 3 minutes, stirring occasionally. Drain and set aside.

2. In a wok over medium-high heat, pour in the peanut oil, swirling to coat the entire surface. Heat the oil for 1 minute and add the garlic, stir-frying for 1 minute, or until golden brown. Add oyster sauce, sugar, black pepper, salt, hoisin sauce, and light soy sauce and stir-fry for 1 minute. Follow with the noodles and mix together for 30 seconds. Remove from heat and set aside to cool. In a mixing bowl, combine cilantro, mint, carrots, and lettuce and set aside.

3. Fill a wok or fry pan (at least 12 inches wide) with very warm water (it works well to place the pan over a burner at low heat to keep the water warm). Submerge one rice paper (at a time) in the water for 10 seconds, or until soft. Remove rice paper from water with a slotted spoon and place on a flat surface. Put a portion of noodles, fresh vegetables and shrimp (about ⅓ cup) on the wrapper, approximately 3 inches in from the edge closest to you. Fold both sides in (to keep the contents from falling out), and roll up.

Store in an airtight container until ready to serve (see tip opposite). Serve with Sauce for Spring Roll (see below) and cucumber slices.

Yield: 8 servings (approximately 20 rolls)

Sauce for Spring Roll

½ cup water
1 cup sugar
1 teaspoon sea salt
2 tablespoons vinegar
⅓ cup ground roasted peanuts
1 tablespoon sriracha chili sauce (optional)

Combine water, sugar, salt, and vinegar in a saucepan and bring to a boil, stirring occasionally. Cook for 5 minutes, or until it turns to a syrup. Remove from heat and mix in the ground peanuts and sriracha chili sauce (optional) before serving.

Fresh Spring Roll with Shrimp (Paw Piah Soad)

Appetizers

Pork Satay (Moo Satay)

Skewers of pork or chicken satay, grilled over charcoal, are sold on street corners throughout Thailand!

½ tablespoon madras curry powder
½ cup coconut milk
2 teaspoons sea salt
1 teaspoon turmeric powder
2 teaspoons sugar
1 pound pork loin (cut into long, thin strips about ¼ inch thick)
1 package bamboo skewers (8 inch length; soak in warm water before use)

1. In a mixing bowl, combine madras curry powder, coconut milk, salt, turmeric powder, sugar, and pork strips. Mix thoroughly, place in a covered container, and refrigerate for at least 2 hours.

2. Thread the marinated pork on to the skewers and grill over charcoal at medium-high heat (turning often) for 6 minutes or until thoroughly cooked (use broiler or deep-fryer if charcoal fire is not available). Serve with Peanut Curry Sauce (see below) and Ar Jard Sauce (see opposite).

Yield: 4 servings

Peanut Curry Sauce

1 cup coconut milk
½ tablespoon red curry paste (see recipe on page 164 or use pre-made)
⅓ cup peanut butter
1 tablespoon sugar
1 teaspoon sea salt
1 tablespoon ground peanut

In a wok over medium-high heat, add the coconut milk and red curry paste. Bring to a boil and cook for 2 minutes, stirring often. Add peanut butter, sugar, and salt, and stir until thoroughly mixed. Cook for 3 minutes, or until red oil droplets appear. Remove from heat and sprinkle with ground peanuts. This sauce should be served warm. Peanut Curry Sauce will keep in the refrigerator for 2-3 days.

Ar Jard Sauce

4 tablespoons sugar
1 teaspoon sea salt
4 tablespoons vinegar
2 tablespoons water

⅓ cup thinly-sliced shallot
⅓ cup thinly-sliced cucumber
1 tablespoon sliced red cayenne pepper (or any sliced red pepper)

Combine sugar, salt, vinegar, and water in a saucepan and bring to a boil. Cook for 2 minutes, stirring occasionally. Turn off the heat and allow sauce to cool. In a small bowl, add shallot, cucumber, and red cayenne pepper and pour the sauce over it. Serve with Pork Satay or Pork with Yellow Curry. Ar Jard Sauce (without shallot, cucumber, and cayenne pepper) will keep in the refrigerator for up to 1 month. This sauce should be served cold.

Pork Satay (Moo Satay)

Tapioca Dumpling with Pork (Sakoo Sai Moo)

This delicious appetizer looks like little bundles of pearls after it's steamed!

1 pound ground pork
3 tablespoons brown sugar
1 teaspoon sea salt
½ cup diced yellow onion
⅓ cup chopped cilantro
2 tablespoons light soy sauce
1 teaspoon black soy sauce
1 teaspoon ground white pepper
1 tablespoon fish sauce
½ cup ground roasted peanuts
1 pound bag tapioca pearls (small size)
½ cup hot water

Sakoo Sai Moo before steaming

1. To make the filling, combine ground pork, brown sugar, and salt in a bowl and mix thoroughly. Preheat a wok over medium-high heat and add the pork mixture. Stir-fry until the pork crumbles into small pieces, about 5 minutes. Add onion, cilantro, light soy, black soy, white pepper, fish sauce, and ground peanuts. Stir-fry for 10 minutes (the filling will get thicker and turn dark brown). Remove from heat, drain in a colander, and allow to cool.

2. To make the tapioca dough, rinse tapioca pearls in cold water, drain thoroughly, and place in a bowl. Pour hot water over the tapioca pearls, a little at a time. Gently knead the pearls for 5 minutes to ensure that they're all covered with water and let sit for 5-10 minutes.

3. Make a ball of tapioca pearls (approximately 1½ tablespoons), flatten on your palm and place 1 heaping teaspoon of the pork mixture in the center. Seal the ball so the pork is totally covered with tapioca (will make approximately 25 balls).

4. Get water boiling in a steamer and lay sheets of wax paper on the rack (or brush the rack with oil) to prevent sticking. Place the balls on the rack and steam covered for 15 minutes, or until the balls turn translucent. Remove from steamer, place on a serving platter and drizzle with fried garlic (see opposite). Serve with lettuce leaves, green onion, cilantro, and Thai chilies.

Yield: 8 servings

Fried Garlic

3 tablespoons peanut oil
2 tablespoons finely-minced garlic

Heat oil in a small saucepan over medium-high heat and stir-fry the garlic until golden brown. Remove from heat and allow to cool. Drizzle over Sakoo Sai Moo. Will keep for up to 2 months without refrigeration.

Tapioca Dumpling with Pork (Sakoo Sai Moo)

Mieng Kham

The seven ingredients in this appetizer combine to create an explosion of flavors in each mouthful!

⅓ cup shredded coconut
2 tablespoons diced ginger (remove skin before dicing)
¼ cup diced fresh Thai chilies (can substitute jalapeno or bell peppers)
⅓ cup diced lime or lemon (with the skin on)
⅓ cup roasted unsalted peanuts
⅓ cup diced shallot or onion
2 tablespoons dried shrimp (small or medium size)
1 head iceberg lettuce (cut into quarters)

Note: Cha-ploo leaves (see photo on page 33) are used in Thailand in place of lettuce leaves for Mieng Kham. They're available at some Asian markets and are slightly bitter-tasting, but provide an interesting contrast to the flavors of the other ingredients.

1. In a frying pan without oil over medium-high heat, roast shredded coconut for 3-5 minutes, stirring occasionally. Remove from heat and let cool.

2. Arrange shredded coconut, ginger, Thai chili, lime or lemon, peanuts, shallot, and dried shrimp on a serving platter. This dish is assembled by placing a small amount of each ingredient on a lettuce leaf and then topping with Mieng Kham Sauce (see below). Wrap it up and enjoy it!

Yield: 6 servings

Mieng Kham Sauce

1 teaspoon finely-minced fresh galanga
½ cup water
⅓ cup tamarind concentrate
½ cup palm sugar
1 teaspoon shrimp paste (kapi)
2 teaspoons sea salt

Wrap galanga in aluminum foil and roast over a burner at low heat for 1-2 minutes. In a small saucepan add water, tamarind concentrate, palm sugar, shrimp paste, salt, and roasted galanga. Stir until the palm sugar and shrimp paste are dissolved and let boil for 5 minutes. Remove from heat and allow to cool before serving. This sauce can be made ahead of time and will keep in the refrigerator for up to 3 weeks.

Mieng Kham served on a lettuce leaf

Mieng Kham

Appetizers 61

Thai Lettuce Wraps (Pae Za Pun)

My mom always makes this dish for Thai New Year!

½ pound dried guilin vermicelli rice noodle (small size)
water for boiling rice stick
3 tablespoons minced garlic
3 tablespoons minced ginger
1 tablespoon sea salt
¼ cup light soy sauce
⅓ cup peanut oil
2 tablespoons sugar
½ teaspoon black pepper
½ pound shrimp (peeled and deveined)
½ pound scallops
½ pound pork loin (⅛ inch thick slices)
1 head of lettuce leaves (clean and separate the leaves)
½ cup mint leaves
½ cup chopped cilantro
½ cup sliced green onion

cooking on an electric griddle

1. Combine garlic, ginger, salt, light soy sauce, peanut oil, sugar, and black pepper in a mixing bowl. Mix thoroughly and apply as a marinade to the shrimp, scallops, and pork. Refrigerate for 30 minutes.

2. Bring water to a boil in a soup pot and cook the noodles until soft, approximately 5 minutes. Remove from heat and drain in cold water. Make small bundles of the noodles and place in a covered container to keep moist.

3. Preheat a non-stick pan over medium-high heat or use an electric griddle to cook the pork for 5 minutes, flipping occasionally with a spatula. The scallops and shrimp should cook for approximately 3 minutes.

4. Arrange pork, scallops, and shrimp on a platter, along with the lettuce leaves, mint, cilantro, and green onion. To serve, place noodles, vegetables, and either shrimp, scallops, or pork on a lettuce leaf and top with Tamarind Peanut Sauce (see opposite). Wrap it up and enjoy!

Yield: 6 servings

Tamarind Peanut Sauce

4 tablespoons peanut oil
⅓ cup thinly-sliced shallot
1 cup water
⅓ cup tamarind concentrate
½ cup sugar

1 tablespoon sea salt
1 boiled egg (crumbled)
1 teaspoon ground Thai chili
⅓ cup ground roasted peanuts

1. In a wok over medium-high heat, add the oil, swirling to coat the entire surface. Heat oil for 1 minute and add the shallot, stirring for 1 minute or until golden brown. Remove from heat and set aside.

2. Combine water, tamarind concentrate, sugar, and salt in a saucepan and bring to a boil, stirring occasionally. Cook for 5 minutes or until it turns to a syrup. Add crumbled egg, ground Thai chili, ground roasted peanuts, and fried shallot and mix thoroughly. Remove from heat and allow to cool. Serve with grilled meats, seafood, steamed fish, or chicken.

Lettuce Wraps (Pae Za Pun) featuring shrimp, scallops, and pork

Shrimp on Lemon Grass Skewers (Goong Obe Ta-krai)

Lemon grass stalks are used as skewers in this tasty appetizer!

1½ pounds shrimp (peeled, deveined and tail off; cut into small pieces)
1 tablespoon thinly-sliced kaffir lime leaf
1 egg (beaten)
2 tablespoons tapioca starch
1 tablespoon palm sugar
1 tablespoon green curry paste (see page 163 or use pre-made)
2 tablespoons fish sauce (nam pla)
⅓ cup coconut cream
5 lemon grass stalks

Note: The inner parts of the lemon grass skewers can be eaten after the shrimp is removed from them.

1. In a food processor, combine the shrimp and the rest of the ingredients (except for the lemon grass stalks). Mix thoroughly until it turns to a paste and set aside at room temperature for 15 minutes.

2. To make the skewers, cut ½ inch off each end of the lemon grass stalk and remove the outer 2-3 layers. Cut the thin part of the stalk about 5 inches from the end (this will make 1 skewer). Cut the thick part of each stalk in half lengthwise (this will make 2 more skewers).

3. Scoop about ⅓ cup of the shrimp mixture and wrap it around one of the lemon grass skewers. Pat it in place so it won't fall off the skewer during grilling. Repeat until all of the shrimp mixture is used up.

4. Grill the skewers over a medium-hot charcoal fire for 5 minutes, turning several times so the shrimp is evenly-browned (but not burned). Use a broiler if charcoal fire is not available, but keep the skewers as far away from the flame as possible. Remove from heat and serve with Ar Jard Sauce (see page 77).

Yield: 4 servings (about 12-15 skewers)

Shrimp on Lemon Grass Skewers (Goong Obe Ta-krai

Crispy Rice Noodle (Mee Grob)

My cooking class students really enjoy making this dish because when the noodles hit the hot oil, they puff up big in about a second!

½ pound dried rice vermicelli noodle
peanut oil for deep-frying
1 package firm tofu (14 ounces)
⅓ cup chopped cilantro
2 stalks green onion (cut diagonally into 1 inch lengths)
1 cup bean sprouts
1 cup shredded iceberg lettuce

1. Preheat peanut oil to 400 degrees in a deep-fryer. Test by dropping 1 strand of noodle in the oil, if it puffs up it's ready. Carefully place a small amount of noodles in the hot oil. They will puff up in about 1 second, so have a wire strainer handy to quickly scoop them out of the oil. Drain noodles in a large bowl lined with paper towels and set aside.

2. Drain water from tofu, pat dry with paper towels, and cut in half (lengthwise). Deep-fry in 400 degree oil until golden brown. Remove from heat and drain on paper towels. Cut tofu into ½ inch squares.

3. To serve, toss the noodles with Mee Grob Topping Sauce (see below) until evenly coated. Top with fried tofu, cilantro, green onion, bean sprouts, and lettuce. Serve right away as the noodles do not stay crisp for long after being mixed with the sauce. Fried noodles will keep for 2 weeks in a covered container.

Yield: 4 servings

Mee Grob Topping Sauce

½ cup water
½ cup sugar
2 tablespoons vinegar
2 tablespoons tomato paste
1 tablespoon sriracha chili sauce
1 teaspoon sesame oil
4 tablespoons fish sauce
2 tablespoons thinly-sliced pickled garlic
1 teaspoon roasted sesame seeds

Combine all of the ingredients (except sesame seeds) in a saucepan over high heat and cook for 10 minutes, stirring occasionally. Remove from heat and stir in the roasted sesame seeds. Allow to cool before using. This sauce will keep for up to 1 month in the refrigerator.

Always have plenty of liquid! 4 donuts

Stir fried rice noodle with coconut milk

- 1/4 pound dried thin rice noodle (Soak in water for 15 minutes.) (and drain)
- 1 cup shrimp
- 2 cup coconut milk
- 2 table spoon olive oil
- 1/4 cup chalot (sliced)
- 2 table spoon salted soy bean
- 1 table spoon ketchop
- 2 table spoon sugar
- 1 tea spoon soy sauce
- 2 tablespoon Black sauce
- 1/4 cup chive
- 1/2 cup bean sprout

1- heat a wok over mediem for 1 minute add shalot until brown add shrimp, salted soy bean, sugar, ketchop, soy sauce stir-frying for 1 minute

2- add coconut cook for 2 minutes then add noodle and black sauce keep stir-frying until the sauce liquid get too dry add chive and remove from the heat.

* Served on top with bean sprout

deep-frying noodles

Crispy Rice Noodle (Mee Grob)

Fried Wonton with Pork (Giow Grob Moo)

The wontons may be stuffed with cream cheese if you prefer!

½ pound ground pork
2 tablespoons mushroom soy sauce
½ teaspoon sea salt
1 egg
⅓ cup dried sliced shiitake mushroom (soak in hot water until soft, drain)
1 teaspoon garlic powder
¼ teaspoon freshly-ground black pepper
1 teaspoon corn starch
3 cups peanut oil or vegetable oil for deep-frying
1 package frozen wonton wrappers (medium size; defrost in refrigerator)
1 teaspoon tapioca starch + ⅓ cup water (mix together, microwave for 30-45 seconds and allow to cool)

1. To make the filling, combine pork, mushroom soy sauce, salt, egg, shiitake mushroom, garlic, black pepper, and corn starch in a bowl and mix thoroughly. Cover the bowl and set aside at room temperature until ready to use.

2. Separate the wonton wraps and place 2 teaspoons of the pork mixture in the middle of a wrapper. Brush a small amount of the tapioca glue along 2 sides of the wrapper. Fold the other 2 sides of the wrapper over so they meet and press them together (so the filling doesn't come out during cooking). Repeat until all of the filling is used. You can prepare the wontons ahead of time as they will keep in the refrigerator for 2-3 days in a sealed container (separate the layers of wontons with wax paper so they won't stick together).

3. Preheat oil to 375 degrees. Deep-fry wontons for at least 5 minutes (to make sure the pork is cooked). Remove from oil with a wire strainer and drain on paper towels. Serve with Fried Wonton Dipping Sauce (see below).

Yield: 8 servings (approximately 40-50 wontons)

Fried Wonton Dipping Sauce

½ cup water
½ cup brown sugar
2½ tablespoons tamarind concentrate
2 tablespoons ketchup
1½ teaspoons sea salt
1 teaspoon sriracha chili sauce (optional)

Bring water to a boil in a wok and add brown sugar, tamarind concentrate, ketchup, salt, and sriracha chili sauce. Cook over high heat for 5 minutes or until the mixture turns to a syrup, stirring often to prevent burning. Allow to cool before serving. The sauce will keep up to 1 month in the refrigerator.

Fried Wonton with Pork (Giow Grob Moo)

Son-In-Law Eggs (Kai Luke Koei)

Luke Koei means son-in-law in Thai and it's not clear exactly where the name of this dish came from. Perhaps they were made as a special treat for a son-in-law? In any case, these eggs are very tasty!

2 tablespoons peanut oil
2 tablespoons thinly-sliced shallot
½ teaspoon five spice powder
¼ cup tamarind concentrate
¼ cup water
2 tablespoons sugar
½ teaspoon ground Thai chili
1 teaspoon black soy sauce
2 teaspoons sea salt
8 hard-boiled eggs (remove the shell)
¼ cup chopped cilantro
oil for deep-frying

Note: Five spice powder, along with tamarind concentrate, ground Thai chili, and black soy sauce, is available at most Asian markets.

1. In a wok over medium-high heat, add the oil and swirl to coat the entire surface. Heat the oil for 1 minute and add the shallot. Stir-fry for 1 minute, or until golden brown. Remove from wok and set aside.

2. In the same wok (with the remaining oil) over medium-high heat, add five spice powder, tamarind concentrate, water, sugar, ground Thai chili, black soy sauce, and salt. Stir-fry for 5 minutes. Remove from heat and set aside.

3. Preheat oil in deep-fryer to 375 degrees and deep-fry the hard-boiled eggs for 1 minute, or until light brown. Remove eggs with a wire strainer or slotted spoon and drain on paper towels. Cut eggs in half (lengthwise) and arrange on a plate or serving platter. Top with the five spice-tamarind sauce and garnish with fried shallot and cilantro. Serve with jasmine or sticky rice.

Yield: 4 servings

Son-In-Law Eggs (Kai Luke Koei)

Curry Puff

These mouth-watering golden brown pastry puffs take some time to prepare, but are a favorite finger food sure to please everyone!

2 cups all-purpose flour
¼ tablespoon salt
½ cup peanut or vegetable oil
¼ cup water

To make the dough, sift the flour and salt into a mixing bowl. Pour the oil and water into the bowl and mix thoroughly by hand. The dough should look like very coarse bread crumbs. Form it into a ball and coat the dough with 1 tablespoon oil. Place in a plastic bag (or airtight container) and let the dough rest for 20-30 minutes.

2 tablespoons peanut oil
½ pound ground pork
1 cup diced yellow onion
1 teaspoon sugar
1 teaspoon sea salt
1¼ tablespoons light soy sauce
1 tablespoon madras curry powder
1 cup diced boiled potato

Note: To make vegetarian curry puffs, omit the pork and double the amount of potatoes (2 cups). Reduce cooking time of the yellow onion to 5 minutes.

1. To make the filling, heat a wok over medium-high heat and pour in the peanut oil, swirling to coat the entire surface. Heat the oil for 1 minute and add the ground pork and yellow onion. Stir-fry for 6-8 minutes. Add the rest of the ingredients and stir-fry for 2 minutes. Remove from heat and allow to cool.

2. To assemble the curry puffs, pull off a piece of dough and make a ball about 1½ inches in diameter. Flatten the ball with a rolling pin. Scoop out about 1 tablespoon of the filling and place in the center of the dough. Fold over the dough and seal the edges by pinching them with your fingers or with a fork. Repeat until all the dough and filling is used.

3. Preheat oil to 375 degrees in a deep-fryer or pan. Place several of the curry puffs in the oil and deep-fry for 1-2 minutes, or until golden brown. Use a wire strainer to remove the curry puffs and drain on paper towels. Serve with Sweet and Sour Sauce (see page 53), sprinkled with ground peanuts and sliced cilantro.

Yield: 8 servings (approximately 24 curry puffs)

Curry Puff

Crispy Sarong Appetizer

Thai women often wear a sarong, which is a piece of fabric wrapped around the body. That apparently was the inspiration for the name of this dish, though in this case noodles are wrapped around a meat filling!

½ pound ground pork
½ pound ground chicken (or turkey)
1 egg
1 tablespoon light soy sauce
2 teaspoons sea salt
1 teaspoon sugar
¾ tablespoon garlic powder
1 teaspoon black pepper
water for boiling noodles
1 pound dried imitation egg noodle (small size)
peanut oil for deep-frying

Note: As the name suggests, imitation egg noodles contain no egg, though they resemble egg noodles in color. They're available in several sizes at Asian markets, usually small (thin) or large (thick). See page 39 for a picture of the dried noodles.

1. To make the filling, combine ground pork, ground chicken, egg, light soy sauce, salt, sugar, garlic powder, and black pepper in a food processor (or blender) and mix thoroughly. Transfer from food processor to freezer and chill for 15 minutes (it's easier to work with the filling if it's chilled).

2. Bring water to a boil in a pot and add the egg noodles. Cook for 3 minutes (do not overcook the noodles or they will break apart when you wrap them around the filling). Turn off the heat and use a wire strainer or slotted spoon to transfer the noodles to a bowl lined with wet paper towels (to keep the noodles moist for the next step). Allow to cool for a few minutes.

3. Take one of the noodle bundles, unravel it and divide into approximately 3 long strands. Make a small ball (about 1 tablespoon) of the filling and wrap with one of the egg noodle strands (all of the filling should be covered by noodle). Tuck the end of the noodle into the pork filling and repeat until all of the filling is wrapped-up with noodles.

4. Preheat oil to 375 degrees in a deep-fryer or pan. Place several of the sarong bundles in the oil and deep-fry for 8-10 minutes, or until golden brown. Use a wire strainer to remove the bundles from the oil and drain on paper towels. Serve with Sweet and Sour Sauce (see page 53).

Yield: 6 servings

Crispy Sarong Appetizer

Thai Fish Cakes (Tod Mun Pla)

*These golden brown beauties are a favorite appetizer --
the thinly-sliced lime leaves really give them a special flavor!*

1 pound catfish or walleye fillets (cut into small pieces)
1 tablespoon red curry paste (see page 164 or use pre-made)
2 cloves garlic (minced)
1 egg
1 tablespoon soy sauce
1 tablespoon fish sauce
1 tablespoon cornstarch
2-3 kaffir lime leaves (thinly-sliced)
⅓ cup chopped cilantro
⅓ cup thinly-sliced long beans (can substitute green beans)
3-4 cups peanut oil for deep-frying

Note: In Thailand, Tod Mun is commonly made with featherback fish (pla grai in Thai). Frozen featherback fish is available in many Asian markets and is typically sold as either a whole fish, or processed into a paste for use in Tod Mun.

1. Combine fish, red curry paste, garlic, egg, soy sauce, fish sauce, and corn starch in a food processor and mix until it turns to a paste. Place mixture in a bowl and (using your hands) mix in lime leaves, cilantro, and long beans.

2. Scoop out 3 tablespoons of the fish cake mixture and flatten with your hands into a patty (about 2-3 inches wide by ½ inch thick). Dip your hands in warm water occasionally if they get too sticky when making the patties. Repeat until all of the fish mixture is used.

3. Preheat oil to 375-400 degrees in a deep-fryer or pan. Deep-fry patties for 5 minutes, or until golden brown. Remove from heat and drain on paper towels. Serve with Ar Jard Sauce (see below).

Yield: 4 servings

Ar Jard Sauce

4 tablespoons sugar
1 teaspoon sea salt
4 tablespoons vinegar
2 tablespoons water

⅓ cup thinly-sliced shallot
⅓ cup thinly-sliced cucumber
1 tablespoon ground roasted peanut
1 teaspoon sriracha chili sauce

Combine sugar, salt, vinegar, and water in a saucepan and bring to a boil. Stir constantly for 2 minutes and allow to cool. Place the shallot and cucumber in a small bowl and follow with Ar Jard Sauce. Finish by sprinkling with ground peanuts and sriracha chili sauce.

Thai Fish Cake (Tod Mun Pla)

Fried Chicken Wings (Peek Gai Tod)

These chicken wings are so popular I usually have to make a double batch!

2 tablespoons soy sauce
1 teaspoon black pepper
1½ tablespoons garlic powder
4 tablespoons all purpose flour
2 teaspoons sea salt
1 tablespoon sugar
2 pounds chicken wings (wash thoroughly and dry on paper towels)
peanut oil for deep-frying

1. Combine soy sauce, black pepper, garlic powder, flour, salt, and sugar in a bowl to create a marinade. Apply to the chicken wings and marinate for 30-60 minutes in the refrigerator (covered with plastic wrap).

2. Preheat oil to 375 degrees in a deep-fryer or pan. Fry chicken wings for 10 minutes, or until golden brown. Place the wings on paper towels to drain off excess oil and serve with sweet chili sauce for chicken (available at Asian markets) or Sweet and Sour Sauce (see page 53).

Yield: 4 servings

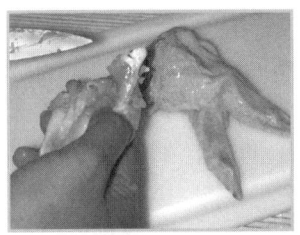

removing bone

stuffing wing

Stuffed Chicken Wings (Peek Gai Yod Sai)

¼ pound ground chicken
⅛ ounce dried bean thread noodle (soak in warm water until soft and drain)
1 clove garlic (minced)
½ teaspoon ground white pepper
2 tablespoons chopped cilantro
¼ cup chopped water chestnut
1 teaspoon light soy sauce
2 tablespoons chopped yellow onion
⅓ cup shredded wood ear mushroom (soak in warm water until soft)
⅓ cup shredded shiitake mushroom (soak in warm water until soft)
8 chicken wings (cleaned)
oil for deep-frying

1. Combine all of the ingredients (except for the chicken wings and oil) in a bowl and mix thoroughly. Make an opening at the top of the chicken wing and roll down the skin and meat. Using a sharp knife, make a cut at the joint to allow the upper bones to be removed. Stuff mixture into the chicken wings through the opening used to remove the bones.

2. Place the stuffed wings in a steamer and steam for 8-10 minutes over medium-high heat. Remove wings from steamer and allow to cool. Deep-fry wings in 375 degree oil for 10 minutes. Remove from oil and drain on paper towels. Serve with Sweet and Sour Sauce (see page 53).

Yield: 4 servings

Pork Toast (Kanom Punk Na Moo)

1 pound ground pork
2 tablespoons minced coriander root (or chopped cilantro)
1 tablespoon minced garlic
2 stalks green onion (thinly-sliced)
½ teaspoon black pepper
1 tablespoon corn starch
4 tablespoons mushroom soy sauce
½ teaspoon sea salt
1 egg
8 slices white or wheat bread (remove crusts and cut into 4 squares)
peanut oil for deep-frying

1. Combine ground pork, coriander root (or cilantro), garlic, green onion, black pepper, corn starch, mushroom soy sauce, salt, and egg in a bowl and mix thoroughly. Spread 1-2 tablespoons of the pork mixture onto each piece of bread and line up on a cookie sheet.

2. Preheat oil to 375 degrees in a deep-fryer or wok. Deep-fry the pork toast for 6 minutes. Remove from heat and drain on paper towels. Serve with Ar Jard Sauce (see page 77).

Yield: 6-8 servings (makes about 32 pieces)

Crab Roll (Hoy Jaw)

Crab Roll (Hoy Jaw) is made with tofu sheets, which are paper-thin pieces of dried tofu. Crab meat and pork are rolled-up and steamed, then deep-fried, and served with plum sauce and hot mustard!

1 pound lump crab meat (can use fresh, frozen, or canned crab meat)
½ pound ground pork
1 egg (beaten)
2 tablespoons corn starch
1 teaspoon freshly-ground white pepper
2 tablespoons light soy sauce
2 tablespoons mushroom soy sauce
1 tablespoon sugar
3 tablespoons oyster sauce
2 dried flat tofu sheets (soak in warm water until soft)
peanut oil for deep-frying
plum sauce
hot mustard

Note: Dried tofu sheets, as well as plum sauce and hot mustard, are available at most Asian markets. It may be possible to find frozen tofu sheets at some Asian markets.

1. Combine crab meat, ground pork, egg, corn starch, white pepper, light soy sauce, mushroom soy sauce, sugar, and oyster sauce in a bowl and mix thoroughly.

2. Pat dry the tofu sheet with paper towel and place on a flat surface. Spoon crab meat mixture along one edge of the sheet. Roll the tofu sheet until round, about 1½ to 2 inches in diameter, and tie with a string (to keep from unrolling).

3. Bring water to a boil in a steamer. Place crab roll on tray and steam covered for 10 minutes. Remove from steamer and allow to cool.

4. Preheat oil in deep-fryer or pan to 375 degrees. Deep-fry crab rolls for 5 minutes. Remove from deep-fryer, drain on paper towels, and remove the string. Cut into ½ inch thick slices and place on a serving platter with lettuce and tomatoes. Serve with plum sauce and hot mustard, or sweet and sour sauce (see page 53).

Yield: 4 servings

Chicken in Pandan Leaves (Gai Hor Bai-toey)

Pandan leaves (bai-toey in Thai) add a wonderful flavor to the chicken during steaming!

⅓ cup coconut cream
2 cloves garlic (minced)
2 tablespoons minced lemon grass
1 tablespoon curry powder
½ teaspoon ground white pepper
2 tablespoons light soy sauce
2 tablespoons fish sauce (nam pla)
1½ teaspoons rice flour
1 teaspoon sesame oil
1 teaspoon sea salt
1 teaspoon rice cooking wine
2 pounds boneless skinless chicken thighs (cut each thigh in half)
pandan leaves for wrapping (available frozen; wash thoroughly before using)
toothpicks (to secure the bundles)

pandan leaf bundles in steamer

1. Combine coconut cream, garlic, lemon grass, curry powder, white pepper, light soy sauce, fish sauce, rice flour, sesame oil, salt, and cooking wine in a bowl to create a marinade. Apply to the chicken and refrigerate for 30-60 minutes.

2. Wrap one piece of marinated chicken in a pandan leaf (start wrapping from the wide end of the pandan leaf towards the pointy end) and secure with a toothpick. Repeat until all of the chicken is wrapped-up.

3. Bring water to a boil in a steamer. Place the pandan leaf bundles on a tray and steam at medium-high heat for 10 minutes. Remove bundles from steamer and set aside.

4. Preheat oil in deep-fryer to 375 degrees. Deep-fry the steamed bundles for 5 minutes. Remove from oil, drain on paper towels, and place bundles on a serving platter (be sure to discard toothpicks and pandan leaves before eating). Serve with Gai Hor Bai-toey Sauce (see opposite) or chili sauce for chicken (available at Asian markets).

Yield: 4 servings

Gai Hor Bai-toey Sauce

1½ cups sugar + 2 tablespoons
1 teaspoon sea salt
½ cup vinegar
½ cup water
1 clove garlic (minced)
2 fresh Thai chilies (minced; can substitute 1 teaspoon chili garlic sauce available at Asian markets)

Combine sugar, salt, vinegar, and water in a saucepan over high heat and bring to a boil. Cook for 5 minutes, stirring occasionally. Add garlic and fresh Thai chilies (or chili garlic sauce) and stir to mix. Remove from heat and allow to cool before serving. Will keep in the refrigerator for 1 month.

Chicken in Pandan Leaves (Gai Hor Bai-toey)

Green Papaya Salad (Som Tum Thai)

Som Tum is traditionally made using a mortar and pestle (or kloke in Thai). If you don't have a kloke, mince the Thai chili and garlic and combine all of the ingredients in a mixing bowl.

1 pound green papaya
2 Thai chilies (add more pepper if you want it hotter!)
1 small clove of garlic
2 strings long bean (cut into 1 inch lengths)
1 tablespoon chopped roasted peanut
5 cherry tomatoes (cut in half)
1 tablespoon palm sugar (or brown sugar)
2 tablespoons lime juice
1½ tablespoons fish sauce (nam pla)
1 teaspoon chopped dried shrimp

1. Cut papaya in half (lengthwise) and remove seeds. Peel the skin of the papaya and shred the flesh using a shredder or knife (the shreds should be thin and long). In a mortar and pestle, pound the chilies and garlic until they're broken up. Add the long beans and roasted peanuts, pounding only enough to break them up a little bit.

2. Add the shredded papaya, tomato, sugar, lime juice, fish sauce, and dried shrimp, pounding until everything is thoroughly mixed together. This dish should taste sweet, sour, and a little bit salty, so you may need to add more sugar, lime juice, or fish sauce to get the taste you like. Som Tum is commonly served with roasted or grilled meats, fried fish, sticky rice, Kao Mun Gai (see page 122), and fresh cabbage or lettuce.

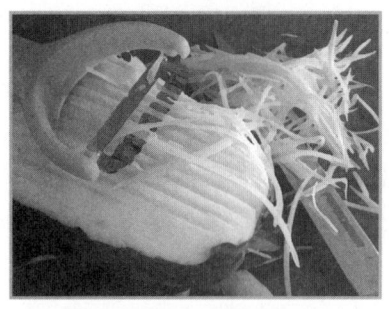

Yield: 4 servings

shredding papaya

Green Papaya Salad (Som Tum Thai) served with kao mun and cabbage

Isaan-style Papaya Salad (Som Tum Pla Ra)

In Thailand, numerous contests are held to see who can eat the spiciest Som Tum, and who can perform the best dance while making it! The Som Tum dance is called tar-tum in Thai and it's done while pounding the mortar and pestle. These contests are so popular that they're often shown on television! So you can see how much Thai people love cooking, dancing, and eating!

1 pound green papaya
2 cloves garlic
10 fresh Thai chili peppers
4 strings long bean (cut into 1 inch lengths; can substitute with 4 ounces of green beans)
5 cherry tomatoes (cut in half)
1 tablespoon lime juice
1 tablespoon fish sauce (nam pla)
2 tablespoons fermented fish sauce (pla ra)
½ teaspoon sugar
½ bulb pickled garlic

Note: Fermented fish sauce (pla ra) differs from regular fish sauce because it's not clear and has a brownish-grey color. Pla ra, along with green papaya, Thai chili, long bean, and pickled garlic, is available at most Asian markets.

1. Cut papaya in half (lengthwise) and remove the seeds. Peel the skin of the papaya and shred the flesh using a shredder or knife (the shreds should be thin and long).

2. In a mortar and pestle, pound the garlic and Thai chilies until coarsely ground. Add the long bean and pound just until it's bruised. Follow with the shredded green papaya, tomato, lime juice, fish sauce, pla ra, sugar, and pickled garlic and pound it all together until thoroughly mixed. Place on a platter and serve with cabbage, fried pork skins, Gai Yang (grilled chicken) and sticky rice.

Yield: 4 servings

ingredients for Som Tum Pla Ra

Isaan-style Papaya Salad (Som Tum Pla Ra)

Northeast Chicken Salad (Laab Gai Isaan)

Laab is a traditional dish of Northeast Thailand that can be made with any kind of ground meat (or mushrooms or tofu). It's usually served with sticky rice and lots of fresh vegetables!

1 pound ground chicken (or turkey)
3 medium-sized shallots (thinly-sliced)
⅓ cup chopped cilantro
½ lime (cut into wedges for easy squeezing)
2 tablespoons roasted rice powder (kao kua in Thai)
2 tablespoons fish sauce (nam pla)
1 teaspoon ground Thai chili (optional)
⅓ cup mint leaves

Note: Roasted rice powder (kao kua in Thai) is available at Asian markets or you can easily make your own. Roast ⅓ cup uncooked sticky rice (or long grain rice) in a frying pan over medium heat without oil for approximately 10 minutes (or until it turns dark brown). Stir the rice often to prevent burning. Grind the roasted rice in a mortar and pestle (or coffee grinder) until it turns to a powder.

1. Cook ground chicken (or turkey) in a wok over medium-high heat for 8 minutes, or until done. Stir often to prevent burning. Drain and set aside to cool.

2. Combine the cooked chicken, shallot, cilantro, juice from the lime, roasted rice powder, fish sauce, and ground Thai chili (optional) in a bowl and mix thoroughly. You may need to adjust the amount of fish sauce (salty flavor) and lime juice (sour flavor) in the recipe to suit your taste.

3. Garnish with mint leaves and serve with sticky rice and plenty of fresh vegetables such as lettuce leaves, cabbage, cilantro, green onion, sliced cucumber, and fresh chili pepper.

Yield: 4 servings

Isaan-style Chicken Salad (Laab Gai) served on lettuce leaves

Grilled Salmon Salad (Laab Pla Salmon)

The flavor of grilled salmon is jazzed-up with galanga, lime leaves, and roasted rice powder!

1 pound salmon fillet
1 tablespoon minced galanga
4 kaffir lime leaves (thinly-sliced)
⅓ cup thinly-sliced shallot
2 tablespoons roasted rice powder (kao kua in Thai; see page 88 or use pre-made)
3 tablespoons lime juice
3 tablespoons fish sauce (nam pla)
1 tablespoon ground Thai chili
2 tablespoons sliced pac peow (bai prik ma in Thai)
⅓ cup chopped cilantro
mint leaves for garnish
½ head lettuce
1 cucumber (sliced)

1. Preheat charcoal in grill to medium-high heat. Grill salmon fillet for 10 minutes (use broiler if charcoal fire is not available).

2. In a mixing bowl, crumble the grilled salmon into fairly small pieces. Add galanga, lime leaves, shallot, roasted rice powder, lime juice, fish sauce, and ground Thai chili. Toss ingredients to thoroughly mix.

3. Add pac peow and cilantro and give it a final toss. Arrange lettuce and cucumber slices on a serving platter and follow with salmon salad. Garnish with mint leaves and serve with sticky rice or jasmine rice.

Yield: 4 servings

Grilled Salmon Salad (Laab Pla Salmon)

Silver Bean Thread Noodle Salad (Yum Woon Sen)

Bean thread noodles provide a nice chewy texture to this delicious salad!

¼ pound ground pork
¼ pound dried silver bean thread noodle (cellophane noodles)
½ pound shrimp (peeled and deveined, with the tail-off)
2 tablespoons chopped pickled garlic
⅓ cup thinly-sliced purple onion
1 tablespoon chopped fresh Thai chili
2-3 tablespoons fresh lemon juice
1 tablespoon sugar
1 teaspoon soyabean paste with chili (nam prik pao)
3-4 tablespoons fish sauce (nam pla)
¼ cup chopped Chinese celery (can substitute regular celery)
⅓ cup chopped cilantro
2 tablespoons chopped roasted peanuts

1. Fill a saucepan with water and bring to a boil. Add ground pork and cook for 6-8 minutes, stirring to break up the pork pieces. Drain and set aside.

2. Fill another saucepan with water and bring to a boil. Add the bean thread noodles and cook for 2 minutes, stirring to break apart the bundles. Add the shrimp and cook for 3 minutes, stirring occasionally. Remove from heat and drain in cold water for a few seconds.

3. In a mixing bowl, combine cooked pork, bean thread noodle, shrimp, and the rest of the ingredients (except peanuts), and toss gently to mix. Sprinkle with roasted peanuts and serve with lettuce and tomato slices.

Yield: 4 servings

Pork Salad with Ginger (Nam Soad)

In Thailand, Nam Soad is often served as an appetizer with cold drinks.

1 teaspoon peanut oil
10 dried Thai chilies (optional)
1 pound ground pork
1 teaspoon sea salt
2 tablespoons lime juice
2 teaspoons sugar
2 tablespoons fish sauce (nam pla)
2 tablespoons shredded ginger (peel the skin before shredding)
⅓ cup chopped cilantro
3 medium-sized shallots (thinly-sliced)
⅓ cup roasted peanuts

1. Heat a small frying pan over medium heat and add peanut oil and dried chilies. Stir constantly for 1-2 minutes. Remove from heat and set aside.

2. Bring water to a boil in a pot and add the ground pork. Cook for 6-8 minutes, or until done. Drain and set aside to cool. Combine cooked ground pork and salt in a bowl and mix thoroughly. Add lime juice, sugar, fish sauce, ginger, cilantro, and shallots and toss until thoroughly mixed.

3. Top with roasted peanuts and fried dried chilies (optional). Serve with lettuce leaves. The flavors of this dish are sour, salty, and sweet so you may need to adjust lime juice, fish sauce, or sugar accordingly.

Yield: 4 servings

Squid Salad (Yum Pla Meuk)

A friend of mine used to love deep-fried squid (calamari), but after she tasted my squid salad she fell in love with it and I had to make it for her every time we got together. It's definitely one of my all-time favorite dishes!

1 pound squid
2 tablespoons chopped pickled garlic
⅓ cup thinly-sliced yellow or purple onion
3 tablespoons fish sauce (nam pla)
1 teaspoon sugar
4 tablespoons lime juice
1 tablespoon minced fresh Thai chili
⅓ cup chopped cilantro
lettuce leaves

1. Clean squid thoroughly and cut along one edge so that it's open. Make shallow cross-hatch cuts on the inside of the skin only (see below, this will make the squid curl up when cooked and leave a nice pattern on the skin).

2. Bring water to a boil in a saucepan, and cook the squid for 3 minutes. Remove from heat, drain, and set aside.

3. Combine the cooked squid, pickled garlic, onion, fish sauce, sugar, lime juice, Thai chili, and cilantro in a bowl. Toss until mixed thoroughly. Place squid salad on a serving platter with lettuce leaves and sprinkle with cilantro. Serve right away or serve cold as an appetizer, along with lettuce and celery.

Yield: 4 servings

inside skin of squid with shallow cross-hatch cuts before cooking

squid curled-up after cooking

Squid Salad (Yum Pla Meuk)

Crispy Catfish with Green Mango (Yum Pla Duke Foo)

Thai people love to eat sour fruits with dipping sauce! In Thailand we have motorcycle fruit men, who drive around the countryside with a glass case containing a variety of fresh and pickled sour fruits with dipping sauces! Yum Pla Duke Foo is one of the most popular ways to eat sour green mango!

1 pound catfish fillets
peanut oil for deep frying
⅓ cup thinly-sliced shallots
¼ cup thinly-sliced lemon grass
1 tablespoon soyabean with chili paste (nam prik pow)
1 tablespoon palm sugar
3 tablespoons fish sauce (nam pla)
3 tablespoons lime juice
1 cup shredded green mango
1 tablespoon sliced fresh Thai chilies
⅓ cup chopped cilantro
⅓ cup mint leaves
⅓ cup roasted peanuts with skin-on

Note: When selecting green mango (available at Southeast Asian markets), try to find very firm, smooth-skinned fruit; it will be crunchier and easier to shred!

1. Preheat oven to 400 degrees and bake catfish fillets for 10 minutes. Remove from oven and allow to cool.

2. Crumble the catfish with a potato masher (or fork) and deep-fry in peanut oil at 400 degrees for 8 minutes, or until golden brown. Use a wire strainer or slotted spoon to scoop out the catfish, drain on paper towels and set aside.

3. Combine shallots, sliced lemongrass, soyabean paste with chili, palm sugar, fish sauce, lime juice, green mango, and Thai chilies in a bowl, tossing to mix thoroughly.

4. Place the fried catfish on a plate and top with the green mango salad mixture. Sprinkle with cilantro, mint leaves, and roasted peanuts. Serve as an appetizer with cold drinks.

Yield: 4 servings

Crispy Catfish with Green Mango (Yum Pla Duke Foo)

Lemon Grass Salad (Yum Ta-krai)

Ta-krai is Thai for lemon grass, and this salad is a great way to enjoy the delicate, citrusy flavor of this delicious herb!

8-10 stalks lemon grass
6 tablespoons palm sugar (or brown sugar)
3 tablespoons fish sauce (nam pla)
¼ cup olive oil
6 tablespoons lime juice
⅓ cup thinly-sliced shallot (or purple onion)
1 tablespoon chopped fresh Thai chili (or serrano chili)
2 cups sliced lettuce
1 cup roasted cashews
⅓ cup mint leaves
⅓ cup chopped cilantro

1. Cut off the woody tops and bottoms of the lemon grass. Remove the outer 2-3 layers and cut the tender middle section diagonally into thin slices.

2. In a mixing bowl, combine palm sugar (or brown sugar), fish sauce, olive oil, and lime juice and stir until the sugar dissolves. Add the lemon grass, shallot (or purple onion), and Thai chili (or serrano chili), and toss until thoroughly mixed. Place lettuce on a serving platter and cover with lemon grass salad. Top with roasted cashews, mint leaves, and cilantro. Serve right away!

Yield: 4 servings

Waterfall - Grilled Pork Salad (Plar Moo Nam Toke)

The name Waterfall refers to the juices that drip off the meat during grilling!

1 pound boneless country-style pork ribs
1 teaspoon sea salt
3 tablespoons lime juice
2 teaspoons ground Thai chili
2 tablespoons roasted rice powder (see page 88, or use pre-made)
3 tablespoons fish sauce (nam pla)
4 tablespoons thinly-sliced shallot (or purple onion)
1 stalk green onion (sliced)
2 tablespoons chopped culantro leaves (pak chee farang in Thai)
2 tablespoons thinly-sliced lemon grass (use only the tender middle part)
lettuce leaves and cucumber slices
⅓ cup mint leaves

1. Thoroughly wash the pork ribs, sprinkle with salt, and refrigerate for 15 minutes. Grill over charcoal at medium-high heat for 10-15 minutes, turning occasionally to prevent burning (if the pork is still pink, cook for 2-3 more minutes). Remove from grill and cut into paper-thin slices.

2. In a mixing bowl, combine the grilled pork, lime juice, Thai chili, roasted rice powder, fish sauce, shallot, and lemon grass and mix thoroughly. Add onion and culanto and toss until mixed. Place lettuce leaves and cucumber slices on a serving platter and follow with grilled pork salad. Top with mint leaves and serve with sticky rice.

Yield: 4 servings

Noodle Soup with Beef (Kuay-tiaw Nua)

*Kuay-tiaw (Noodle soup) is eaten every day in Thailand.
Sold on the street everywhere, it's a cheap, delicious, nutritious meal.*

8 cups water
1 pound beef soup bone
¼ pound daikon radish (cut into 4 inch lengths)
1 bruised ginger root (3 inch length)
1 tablespoon sea salt
1 teaspoon black peppercorn
3 pieces star anise
4 medium-sized shallots (peel-off skin)
1 pound beef chuck roast (thinly-sliced)
1 pound fresh rice stick noodle (cut into 5 inch lengths)
½ pound bean sprouts
1 medium-sized yellow onion (thinly-sliced)

1. In a soup pot, bring water to a boil and add beef soup bone, daikon radish, ginger, and salt. Wrap the peppercorns, star anise, and shallots in cheesecloth (or a coffee filter) and immerse in the boiling water. Let it boil for at least 10-15 minutes, being sure to skim off any foam floating on the surface. Place the thinly-sliced beef in a wire strainer and submerge in the boiling broth for 3 minutes, stirring constantly, then set aside.

2. In a small soup pot, bring several cups of water to a boil. Add the noodles and cook for 10 seconds, drain, and divide into 4 large soup bowls. Place cooked beef slices on top of the noodles and sprinkle with bean sprouts and onion. Season the soup with the various condiments (see below) and cover with the steaming broth. Mix all the ingredients together with chopsticks and spoon. Kuay-tiaw should be served with fresh vegetables such as lettuce, mint, culantro, Thai basil, and Thai chili.

Yield: 4 servings

Condiments (per bowl)

1 teaspoon hoisin sauce
2 teaspoons fish sauce (nam pla)
1 teaspoon sriracha chili sauce
2 teaspoons sugar
½ teaspoon fried garlic (see page 59 or purchase at Asian market)

½ teaspoon lime juice
1 teaspoon sliced green onion
1 teaspoon chopped cilantro
½ teaspoon ground Thai chili
¼ teaspoon black or white pepper

Noodle Soup with Beef (Kuay-tiaw Nua)

Thai Hot and Sour Shrimp Soup (Tom Yum Goong)

Perhaps the most famous of all Thai soups, Tom Yum is a rich, spicy, sour, salty, sweet treat in a bowl!

6 cups water
4 slices galanga (⅛ th inch thick)
1 stalk lemon grass (cut into 1 inch lengths)
4 medium-sized shallots (remove skin)
1 tablespoon sea salt
1 can whole straw mushrooms (15 ounces, drain off the water; can substitute with 1 cup sliced fresh white mushrooms)
5 kaffir lime leaves
½ teaspoon sugar
1 tablespoon soyabean paste with chili (nam prik pow)
3 tablespoons fish sauce (nam pla)
1 tablespoon tamarind soup base powder
1 pound black tiger shrimp (peeled and deveined, but leave the tail on)
3 fresh Thai chilies (bruised, optional)
3 stalks green onion (cut into 1 inch lengths)
1 tablespoon lime juice
⅓ cup sliced cilantro (1 inch lengths)

Note: galanga, straw mushrooms, lime leaves, soyabean paste with chili, tamarind soup base powder, and Thai chilies are available at most Asian markets.

1. Bring water to a boil in a soup pot. Add galanga, lemon grass, shallot, and salt and let boil for 3 minutes, stirring occasionally.

2. Add mushrooms, lime leaves, sugar, soyabean paste, fish sauce, and tamarind soup base powder. Stir to mix and let boil for 2 minutes.

2. Stir in the shrimp, Thai chilies, and green onion and cook for 3 minutes. Remove from heat and add the lime juice and cilantro, stirring until mixed (the lemon grass, galanga, lime leaves and shallot are used only for flavoring and should be discarded before serving). Serve hot with jasmine rice.

Yield: 4 servings

Thai Hot and Sour Shrimp Soup (Tom Yum Goong)

Chicken and Coconut Milk Soup (Tom Kha Gai)

A famous Thai soup, Tom Kha Gai features the flavors and aromas of coconut, galanga, lemon grass, and lime leaves!

2 cups water
4 slices galanga (⅛ th inch thick)
1 stalk lemon grass (cut into 1 inch lengths)
2 kaffir lime leaves
2 medium-sized shallots (sliced)
2 teaspoons sea salt
1 teaspoon sugar
1 pound boneless skinless chicken breast (cut into bite-sized pieces)
1 can oyster mushrooms (15 ounces; drain off water and cut into bite-sized pieces)
1 can coconut milk (13.5 ounces)
2 fresh Thai chilies (minced)
2 stalks green onion (cut into 1 inch lengths)
3 tablespoons fish sauce (nam pla)
1-2 tablespoons lime juice
¼ cup sliced cilantro (1 inch lengths)

1. Bring water to a boil in a soup pot. Add galanga, lemon grass, lime leaves, shallot, salt, and sugar. Boil for 2 minutes, stirring occasionally.

2. Add chicken, oyster mushrooms, and coconut milk. Bring to a boil and cook for 6-8 minutes, stirring occasionally.

3. Add Thai chilies, green onion, fish sauce, and lime juice and stir until mixed. Remove from heat and garnish with cilantro leaves (the galanga, lemon grass and lime leaves are used only for flavoring and should be discarded before serving). Serve with fried rice or jasmine rice. This dish may be served as an appetizer or a main dish.

Yield: 4 servings

Chicken and Coconut Milk Soup (Tom Kha Gai)

Clear Noodle Soup with Tofu (Gang Jeud Woon Sen)

Gang Jeud Woon Sen is a very simple, clear soup. I usually make it once a week and it's truly a comfort food to me; it helps my stomach relax after eating spicy food all week!

¼ pound dried silver bean thread noodle
8 cups water
¼ pound daikon radish (cut into ½ inch slices)
1 tablespoon sea salt
1 package tofu (14 ounces; drain off water and cut into cubes)
⅓ cup chopped Chinese celery (can substitute regular celery)
⅓ cup thinly-sliced yellow onion
3 tablespoons mushroom soy sauce
1 teaspoon sugar
½ teaspoon black pepper
15 pieces dried lily flowers (soak in warm water for 3 minutes and tie in a knot)
1 tablespoon chopped cilantro
1 tablespoon fried garlic (see page 58 or use pre-made)

Note: A variety of fresh and dried tofu, as well as Chinese celery, mushroom soy sauce, dried lily flowers, and fried garlic is available at most Asian markets.

1. Soak bean thread noodle in hot water until soft, approximately 5 minutes. Drain noodles, cut into 5 inch lengths, and set aside.

2. Bring water to a boil in a soup pot and add daikon and salt. Cook until the daikon is soft, approximately 5 minutes.

3. Add tofu, Chinese celery, onion, mushroom soy sauce, sugar, black pepper, dried lily flowers, and bean thread noodles. Cook for 2 minutes, stirring until the ingredients are mixed. Turn off the heat and stir in cilantro and fried garlic. Serve hot or warm.

Yield: 4 servings

Wonton Soup with Pork (Gio Nam Moo)

Wonton Soup is comfort food in any language!

8 cups water
1 pound pork bones
1 medium-sized whole yellow onion (remove skin)
1 tablespoon sea salt
1 stalk Chinese celery (cut into 1 inch lengths; can substitute regular celery)
½ pound ground pork
⅓ cup sliced green onion
¼ teaspoon black pepper
3 tablespoons light soy sauce
½ tablespoon minced garlic
1 teaspoon sugar
1 tablespoon corn starch
1 package wonton wrappers (medium size)
1 egg (beaten)
⅓ cup chopped cilantro
1 tablespoon fried garlic (see page 58 or use pre-made)

1. In a soup pot, bring water to a boil and add the pork bones, onion, salt, and Chinese celery. Boil for 15 minutes, reduce to simmer, and keep warm until ready for use (skim off the foam before ladling into bowls).

2. Combine ground pork, green onion, black pepper, light soy sauce, garlic, sugar, and corn starch in a bowl and mix thoroughly.

3. Spoon approximately 1 teaspoon of the pork mixture into the middle of a wonton wrapper. Brush a small amount of the beaten egg along 2 sides of the wrapper. Fold the other 2 sides of the wrapper over so they meet and press them together. Repeat until all of the filling is used (should make 25-30 pieces).

4. Bring more water to a boil and cook the stuffed wontons for 5 minutes. Remove from heat, scoop out the wontons with a strainer or slotted spoon, and place in a soup bowl. Cover with hot soup broth and sprinkle with chopped cilantro and fried garlic. Serve hot.

Yield: 6 servings

Sour Curry Soup with Shrimp (Gang Som Goong)

*Gang Som is a very common soup in Thai home cooking. I remember during the rainy season, my dad and brothers would go fishing for mudfish (pla chon) and catfish (pla duke). On the way home they would pick wild vegetables like red water lily (sai bua dang), water spinach (pak boong), and water mimosa (pak kra-chet). Then my mom would make fresh vegetables with dipping sauce (Nam Prik Pak Soad) and of course Gang Som Pla Chon Sai Bua (Sour Curry Soup with Mudfish and Red Water Lily)!
It's one of my all-time favorites!*

sour curry paste (use entire recipe below or use ⅓ cup pre-made sour curry paste available at Asian markets)
5 cups water
¼ pound cauliflower (cut into small pieces)
2 tablespoons sea salt
2 stalks celery (cut into 1 inch lengths)
⅓ cup tamarind concentrate
1 tablespoon sugar
¼ pound Chinese cabbage (also called napa; cut into 2 inch lengths)
1 pound black tiger shrimp (peeled and deveined, with tail left on)
¼ pound smoked salmon or smoked herring fillet (crumbled)

1. In a soup pot, bring sour curry paste and water to a boil. Add the cauliflower, salt, celery, tamarind concentrate, and sugar and cook for 3 minutes, stirring occasionally.

2. Add Chinese cabbage, shrimp, and smoked salmon (or herring) and cook for 3 minutes, stirring occasionally. Remove from heat and serve hot with jasmine rice.

Yield: 4 servings

Sour Curry Paste (Nam Prik Gang Som)

3 dried chili pops (remove seeds and soak in hot water for 3 minutes, scoop out paste from the chilies and discard the skins)
2 dried Thai chilies
3 tablespoons minced shallot
1 tablespoon shrimp paste (kapi)

1½ tablespoons chopped krachai (about 2 roots)
1 ginger root (about 4 inches long; remove skin and chop)
2 cloves garlic (minced)

Note: chili pop, krachai (also called rhizome), and shrimp paste are available at most Asian markets.

Combine all of the ingredients in a food processor (or mortar and pestle) and mix until it turns to a paste. If using a mortar and pestle, pound the hard ingredients first, then add chili pop and shrimp paste at the end. Use the entire recipe for Sour Curry Soup with Shrimp (Gang Som Goong). Will keep in the refrigerator for up to 1 week.

Hot and Sour Soup (Gang Som Goong)

Pumpkin Coconut Soup (Fak Tong Gang Ka Ti)

Since the skin of the pumpkin squash is edible, I like to use a shredder to leave a little bit of the skin on, which leaves a nice design!

2 cups water
1 pound pumpkin squash (also called kabocha or Japanese squash; cut in half to remove seeds, peel the skin, and cut into bite-sized pieces)
1 tablespoon minced galanga
1 tablespoon minced lemon grass
2 tablespoons chopped shallot
1 tablespoon sea salt
2 fresh Thai chilies (minced)
5 kaffir lime leaves
1 can coconut milk (13.5 ounces)
3 stalks green onion (cut into 1½ inch lengths)
½ cup lemon basil (bai maengluck; if fresh is not available, substitute dried or frozen)

1. In a soup pot over high heat, bring water to a boil. Add pumpkin, galanga, lemon grass, shallot, salt, Thai chilies, and lime leaves. Cook over high heat until the pumpkin is soft, approximately 5 minutes.

2. Add coconut milk and green onion and let boil for 2 minutes, stirring occasionally. Turn off the heat and stir in lemon basil. Serve hot.

Yield: 4 servings

Rice Soup with Pork (Kao Tom Moo)

In Thailand, Rice Soup is often eaten late at night at one of the many shops selling this original Thai comfort food. In the home, it's usually eaten for breakfast.

1 pound ground pork
1 teaspoon ground white pepper
1 teaspoon sea salt
6 cups pork broth (see page 113)
4 cups cooked jasmine rice (see page 116)
3 tablespoons light soy sauce
⅓ cup chopped Chinese celery
2 stalks green onion (sliced)
2 tablespoons fried garlic (see page 59 or use pre-made)

1. Combine ground pork, white pepper, and salt in a bowl, mix thoroughly and set aside. In a soup pot, bring pork broth to a boil. Using a teaspoon, scoop up seasoned ground pork and drop it into the broth, one scoop at a time. Cook over high heat for 6 minutes, stirring occasionally.

2. Add cooked jasmine rice, light soy sauce, Chinese celery, green onion, and fried garlic and stir for 1 minute. Serve hot with chili vinegar (optional; see page 159).

Yield: 4 servings

Soup base ingredients (shown above): center, white peppercorn; 2nd from center, star anise; 3rd from center, cinnamon stick; clockwise from top, daikon radish; coriander root; ginger; Chinese celery; yellow onion.

Chicken Bone Soup Broth

8 cups water
1 pound chicken bones
¼ pound daikon radish (cut into 4 inch lengths)
2 pieces star anise
1 medium-sized yellow onion (remove skin)
6 pieces coriander root (or ⅓ cup chopped cilantro)
1 tablespoon soy sauce
1 tablespoon sea salt

Bring water to a boil in a soup pan. Add chicken bones, daikon radish, star anise, onion, coriander root, soy sauce, and salt. Cook for 20 minutes over medium-high heat. Remove from heat and strain the broth. Will keep in refrigerator for 3 days or frozen for up to 1 month.

Beef Bone Soup Broth

1 tablespoon white peppercorn
1 cinnamon stick
2 pieces star anise
8 cups water
1 pound beef bones
¼ pound daikon radish (cut into 4 inch lengths)
1 medium-sized yellow onion (remove skin)
1 bruised ginger root (4 inch length)
2 pieces coriander root (or ⅓ cup chopped cilantro)
1 tablespoon sea salt
1 tablespoon light soy sauce

1. Preheat oven to 350 degrees. Wrap white peppercorn, cinnamon stick, and star anise in aluminum foil, roast in oven for 10 minutes, and set aside.

2. Bring water to a boil in a soup pot. Add the white peppercorn, cinnamon stick, star anise, and the rest of the ingredients and cook for for 20 minutes over medium-high heat. Remove from heat and strain the broth. Will keep in refrigerator for 3 days or frozen for up to 1 month.

Pork Bone Soup Broth

8 cups water
1 pound pork bones
1 tablespoon white peppercorn
2 pieces star anise
2 pieces daikon radish (4 inch lengths)
1 medium-sized yellow onion (remove skin)
1 piece ginger (4 inch length, bruised)
1 stalk Chinese celery (cut into 2 inch lengths)
4 pieces coriander root (or ⅓ cup chopped cilantro)
2 tablespoons sea salt

Bring water to a boil in a soup pan. Add pork bones, white peppercorn, star anise, daikon radish, onion, ginger, Chinese celery, coriander root, and salt. Cook for 20 minutes over medium-high heat. Remove from heat and strain the broth. Will keep in refrigerator for 3 days or frozen for up to 1 month.

A Little Bit About Rice

Jasmine Rice (kao homm mali)   Sticky Rice (kao niaw)

An entire cookbook could be written just about rice in Thailand! That's how important it is to the cuisine and culture of Thailand. In fact, if you go to Thailand, you may be asked this question: "kin kao, reu yang?" It means "have you eaten yet?" but "kin kao" actually translates to "eat rice". Rice is very precious to Thai people, so it's never wasted or thrown away. Kids are taught at a very young age not to waste this most important of all Thai foods! Rice is never left uncovered during a meal, and if you go to a restaurant, you're only given as much rice as you can eat.

Rice is used in so many different ways every day of the year. Jasmine rice or sticky rice is eaten with most meals, and in addition, most of the noodles eaten in Thailand are made from rice. Roasted sticky rice is ground into a powder and used to flavor many foods in Northeast Thailand. Rice soup is eaten very often for a late night snack or breakfast dish. Sticky rice is used in many different desserts, including one in which it's placed on a stick and grilled over charcoal! Rice flours are used in many desserts and as a thickener. Rice paper is used to wrap up spring rolls, and fried rice, of course, is yet another example of the many ways this versatile grain is used in Thailand.

Jasmine rice appears translucent before it's cooked, whereas sticky rice (also called glutinous rice) appears to be a solid white color. After cooking, the opposite is true; jasmine rice is white and sticky rice is translucent! Jasmine rice or kao homm mali gets its name from: kao=rice, homm=smell, mali=jasmine flower. Grown for over a hundred years in Thailand, it has a very subtle jasmine-like aroma when cooked that's unique among all kinds of rice. Jasmine rice, as well as sticky rice, is available in 5, 10, 25, or 50 pound bags. There's usually a date on the bag which symbolizes the year of the rice crop, and the newer the rice, the softer it will be.

Sticky rice is primarily eaten in North and Northeast Thailand and many people still eat it the traditional way, by rolling it into a small ball and using it to grab meat, vegetables, and sauces. The method of cooking differs quite a bit from jasmine rice. It must be soaked first and then steamed in a bamboo steaming basket. After it's cooked, the rice is often placed in a woven bamboo serving basket to keep it warm during the meal.

a rice field in Isaan

Jasmine Rice (Kao Homm Mali)

2 cups jasmine rice (rinse in cold water before using)
1½ cups water

1. If you have a rice cooker (highly recommended) you can just add the rice and water and cook.

2. In a saucepan over high heat, add the rice and water and bring to a boil. Cover the pan and cook for 5 minutes. Reduce heat to simmer and cook for 5-10 minutes, or until fluffy (do not stir the rice during cooking). Remove from heat and allow to sit for 5 minutes before serving.

Note: If substituting regular long grain rice, use 2 cups of water.

Yield: 2-4 servings

Sticky Rice (Kao Niaw)

3 cups sticky rice (also called glutinous rice or sweet rice)

Equipment:

Aluminum steamer pot
Bamboo basket for steaming
Bamboo serving baskets

sticky rice steamer pot and bamboo basket

1. Soak sticky rice in cold water overnight or in warm water for at least 3 hours. Transfer the rice to the bamboo steamer basket, allow to drain and set aside.

2. Fill the bottom of the aluminum steamer pot with 6 cups water and bring to a boil. Place the bamboo basket (with the rice) in the steamer pot, cover with any round cover that fits and cook for 10 minutes, or until the rice is translucent. Place the cooked rice in bamboo serving baskets to keep warm while eating.

Yield: 2-4 servings

Thai Fried Rice with Pork (Kao Pad Moo)

Thai Fried Rice is easy to make, and it's a great way to use left-over rice!

¼ cup peanut oil
2 cloves garlic (minced)
1 pound pork loin (cut into bite-sized pieces)
2 eggs (beaten)
1 medium-sized yellow onion (cut in half and sliced)
4 cups cooked long grain rice (see page 116)
4 tablespoons soy sauce
½ teaspoon sea salt
2 teaspoons sugar
1 teaspoon black soy sauce
2 medium-sized tomatoes (cut lengthwise into quarters)
½ teaspoon black pepper

1. Heat a wok over medium-high heat and add peanut oil, swirling to coat the entire surface. Heat oil for 1 minute and add garlic, stir-frying for 1 minute, or until golden brown. Raise the heat to high, add pork loin and stir-fry for 6-8 minutes or until thoroughly cooked.

2. Make a place in the middle of the wok for the beaten eggs and stir-fry for 30 seconds, or until scrambled. Add onion, cooked rice, soy sauce, salt, sugar, and black soy sauce and stir-fry for 4-5 minutes.

3. Finally, add tomatoes and stir gently to mix. Remove from heat, place on a platter and garnish with cilantro leaves and lime wedges. This dish should be served with sliced cucumber, green onions, and Prik Nam Pla (see below).

Yield: 4 servings

Prik Nam Pla (Fish Sauce with Chilies)

4-5 fresh Thai chilies (sliced)
2 tablespoons fish sauce (nam pla)

Combine Thai chilies and fish sauce and place in a small serving dish.

Pineapple Fried Rice with Shrimp

For this recipe, a pineapple is cut in half, the fruit is scooped-out, and the rice is served in the hollowed-out pineapple halves!

4 tablespoons peanut oil
1 tablespoon minced garlic
1 pound black tiger shrimp (peeled and deveined, but tail left on)
⅓ cup diced carrot
⅓ cup diced onion
1 egg (beaten)
4 cups cooked jasmine rice (see page 116)
¼ cup minced prawn in spices (available canned at Asian markets)
2 teaspoons sugar
⅓ cup sweet peas
⅓ cup raisins
2 tablespoons soy sauce
2 tablespoons light soy sauce
1 fresh pineapple (cut in half lengthwise, scoop out pineapple and cut into bite-sized pieces)
⅓ cup roasted cashew nuts

1. Heat a wok over medium-high heat and add peanut oil, swirling to coat the entire surface. Heat oil for 1 minute and add the garlic, stir-frying for 1 minute, or until golden brown. Add the shrimp and stir-fry for 1 minute. Follow with carrot and onion, stir-frying for 2 minutes.

2. Raise heat to high and make a space in the middle of the wok for the beaten egg. Stir egg constantly for 30 seconds, or until scrambled. Add rice, minced prawn in spices, sugar, sweet pea, raisins, soy sauce, light soy sauce, and fresh pineapple. Stir-fry until the ingredients are mixed and thoroughly cooked, approximately 5 minutes.

3. Remove from heat and place fried rice in hollowed-out pineapple halves. Top with cashews and garnish with cilantro before serving.

Yield: 4 servings

Pineapple Fried Rice with Shrimp (served in a hollowed-out pineapple)

Yellow Curry Fried Rice with Shrimp
(Kao Pad Pong Karee)

The curry powder adds a nice flavor to the fried rice, as well as a beautiful yellow color!

¼ cup peanut oil
4 cloves garlic (minced)
1 pound shrimp (peeled and deveined, leave tail on)
1 egg (beaten)
⅓ cup diced carrot
½ cup diced yellow onion
4 cups cooked jasmine rice or long grain rice (see page 116)
⅓ cup sweet peas (fresh or frozen)
2 tablespoons madras curry powder (pong karee in Thai)
⅓ cup coconut milk
1 teaspoon sea salt
1 tablespoon sugar
½ teaspoon black pepper
4 tablespoons light soy sauce

1. Heat a wok over medium-high heat and add peanut oil, swirling to coat the entire surface. Heat oil for 1 minute and add garlic, stir-frying for 1 minute. Add the shrimp and stir-fry for 2 minutes.

2. Raise heat to high and make a space in the middle of the wok for the beaten egg. Stir egg for 30 seconds and follow with carrot and onion, stir-frying for 2 minutes.

3. Add cooked rice, sweet pea, yellow curry powder, coconut milk, salt, sugar, black pepper, and light soy sauce and stir-fry for 4 minutes. Remove from heat, garnish with cilantro leaves and serve hot.

Cooking Tip: It may be helpful for step 3 to combine all of the ingredients in a bowl, so that they can be added to the wok at the same time!

Yield: 4 servings

Yellow Curry Fried Rice with Shrimp (Kao Pad Pong Karee)

Chicken and Rice with Ginger Sauce (Kao Mun Gai)

*Kao Mun Gai is a very simple dish that's easy to make --
the Ginger Sauce gives it a special taste!*

5 cups water
1 tablespoon sea salt
2 whole shallots (remove skin)
4 chicken breasts (with skin and bone intact)
2 cups jasmine rice (uncooked)
⅓ cup cilantro (cut into 1 inch lengths)
1 stalk green onion (cut into 1 inch lengths)
1 cucumber (sliced)

1. In a soup pot over high heat, add water, salt, and shallot and bring to a boil. Add the chicken breasts and cook for 15 minutes over high heat. Turn off the heat and remove the chicken breasts from the pot (reserve the broth for later use). Remove the skin and bone from the chicken breasts and cut the meat into ½ inch thick slices (cut across the breast). Keep the chicken slices in a warm place until ready to serve.

2. To cook the rice, place 1½ cups chicken broth and 2 cups rice in a saucepan over high heat. Bring to a boil and cook for 5 minutes. Lower the heat, cover the pan and cook for 10-15 more minutes, or until the rice is fluffy. Remove from heat and set aside (if you have a rice cooker, you can use it instead of a saucepan to cook the rice).

3. To serve, spoon the rice onto a plate and top with chicken breast slices. Ladle warm Ginger Sauce (see opposite) over the chicken and garnish with cilantro, green onion, and cucumber slices. Serve right away!

Yield: 4 servings

Ginger Sauce

½ cup water (or use leftover broth from boiling the chicken)
2 tablespoons minced ginger
2 cloves garlic (minced)
2 tablespoons soyabean sauce (tow jiew)
½ cup sugar
3 tablespoons vinegar
1 teaspoon black soy sauce
1 teaspoon sea salt
2 fresh Thai chilies (minced)

Bring water (or chicken broth) to a boil in a saucepan. Add the rest of the ingredients and boil for 6 minutes, stirring occasionally. Remove from heat and serve hot or warm. This sauce can be pre-made and will keep in the refrigerator for up to 1 week.

Chicken and Rice with Ginger Sauce (Kao Mun Gai)

Fried Rice Cake with Red Curry (Kao Tod Nam Kluke)

Growing up, one of our family's favorite dishes was Nam Kluke. My mom made it on weekends and everyone loved it! She always served it with lots of fresh vegetables like lettuce, cilantro, green onion, culantro, cha-ploo, and mint.

2 tablespoons red curry paste (see page 164 or use pre-made)
2 teaspoons sea salt
¼ cup water
¼ teaspoon black pepper
⅓ cup grated unsweetened coconut
1 tablespoon tapioca starch
4 cups cooked jasmine rice (see page 116)
6 cups oil for deep-frying
10 deep-fried dried Thai chilies (optional; served on the side)
1 egg (beaten)
2 stalks green onion (thinly-sliced)
2 medium-sized shallots (thinly-sliced)
1 medium-sized yellow onion (thinly-sliced)
1 tablespoon fish sauce (nam pla)
⅓ cup chopped cilantro
1 lime (juiced)

1. Combine red curry paste, salt, water, black pepper, grated coconut, and tapioca starch in a bowl and mix thoroughly. Pour over cooked jasmine rice and use your hands to mix all the ingredients together. Divide the rice mixture into approximately 8 pattycakes (the size of the cakes doesn't matter, but they need to be tightly pressed or they'll fall apart when deep-fried).

2. In a frying pan or deep-fryer, heat the oil to 400 degrees. Dip rice cakes in the beaten egg until covered and deep-fry for 8 minutes, or until golden brown. Drain on paper towels and allow to cool. Deep-fry Thai chilies for 30 seconds and drain (optional).

3. In a large bowl, crumble the deep-fried rice cakes into small pieces and add green onion, shallot, yellow onion, fish sauce, cilantro, and lime juice. Mix thoroughly and serve with fried Thai chilies and fresh vegetables.

Yield: 4-6 servings

Fried Rice Cake with Red Curry (Kao Tod Nam Kluke)

Stir-fried Beef With Holy Basil (Nua Pad Bai Grapow)

Nua Pad Bai Grapow can be stir-fried very quickly -- sometimes I like to add 2 cups of cooked jasmine rice and make fried rice with beef and basil. Otherwise, just serve jasmine rice on the side along with a fried egg!

3 tablespoons peanut oil
4 cloves garlic (minced)
1 pound lean ground beef
1 cup sliced yellow onion
2 banana peppers (sliced into long strips; can substitute with ½ cup sliced green bell pepper)
1 tablespoon minced fresh Thai chili
½ cup holy basil (bai grapow)
1 tablespoon light soy sauce
⅓ cup oyster sauce
1 tablespoon sugar
½ teaspoon black pepper
2 teaspoons soyabean paste (tow jiew in Thai)
⅓ cup water

Note: If fresh holy basil (bai grapow) is not available, substitute with frozen holy basil or fresh Thai basil (bai horapha).

1. Preheat a wok over high heat and add peanut oil, swirling to coat the entire surface. Heat oil for 1 minute and add garlic, stir-frying for 30 seconds. Follow with the ground beef and stir-fry for 5 minutes, or until thoroughly cooked.

2. Add the onion, banana peppers, Thai chili, and holy basil and stir-fry for 2 minutes. Follow with light soy sauce, oyster sauce, sugar, black pepper, soyabean paste, and water and stir-fry for 4 minutes. Remove from heat and serve with jasmine rice, fried egg, and cucumber slices.

Yield: 4 servings

Stir-fried Beef with Holy Basil (Nua Pad Bai Grapow)
served with jasmine rice, fried egg, and cucumber slices

Stir-Fried Sweet and Sour Pork
(Moo Pad Prio Wan)

Fresh pineapple, young ginger, and marinated tender pork are highlighted in this recipe!

2 cloves garlic (minced)
2½ tablespoons light soy sauce
3 tablespoons sugar
1 teaspoon ground white pepper
1 tablespoon cornstarch
1½ tablespoons rice cooking wine
2 tablespoons peanut oil
1 pound pork loin (cut into bite-sized pieces)
1 medium-sized green bell pepper (cut into square pieces)
1 medium-sized yellow onion (cut into square pieces)
½ cup fresh pineapple chunks (can substitute with canned pineapple)
2 tablespoons fresh shredded young ginger (substitute with regular ginger)
⅓ cup ketchup
½ cup pineapple juice
1 tablespoon white vinegar
1 teaspoon black pepper
1 teaspoon sea salt
2 medium-sized tomatoes (cut into quarters)

1. In a mixing bowl, combine minced garlic, 1½ tablespoons light soy sauce, 1 tablespoon sugar, white pepper, cornstarch, and rice cooking wine to create a marinade. Apply to the pork loin and refrigerate for 20-30 minutes.

2. Preheat a wok over high heat and add peanut oil, swirling to coat the entire surface. Heat the oil for 1 minute and add the marinated pork, stir-frying for 6-8 minutes, or until thoroughly cooked.

3. Add green bell pepper, onion, and pineapple and stir-fry for 4-5 minutes. Follow with ginger, ketchup, pineapple juice, vinegar, 1 tablespoon light soy sauce, 2 tablespoons sugar, black pepper, salt, and tomatoes and stir-fry for 1-2 minutes. Remove from heat and serve hot with jasmine rice.

Yield: 4 servings

Sweet and Sour Pork (Moo Pad Prio Wan)

Stir-Fried Pork with Ginger (Moo Pad King)

I love to use Chinese celery in this dish because it's more aromatic than regular celery, especially when cooked with ginger and shiitake mushrooms!

4 tablespoons peanut oil
3 cloves garlic (minced)
1 pound pork loin (cut into bite-sized pieces)
4-5 dried shiitake mushrooms (soak in warm water until soft and cut in half)
1½ cups sliced white mushroom
1 cup sliced yellow onion
1 tablespoon shredded ginger (remove the skin before shredding)
1 stalk Chinese celery (cut into 1 inch lengths; can substitute regular celery)
3 stalks green onion (cut into 1 inch lengths)
1 teaspoon garlic powder
1 tablespoon sugar
⅓ cup oyster sauce
1 tablespoon light soy sauce
1 teaspoon freshly-ground black pepper
1 teaspoon tapioca starch + ⅓ cup water (mix thoroughly)

1. Preheat a wok over medium-high heat and add peanut oil, swirling to coat the entire surface. Heat oil for 1 minute and add the garlic, stir-frying for 1 minute, or until golden brown. Raise the heat to high, add the sliced pork and stir-fry for 8 minutes, or until thoroughly cooked.

2. Make a space in the middle of the wok by moving the pork to the side with a spatula. Add shiitake mushrooms, white mushrooms, onion, ginger, and Chinese celery and stir-fry for 3 minutes. Follow with green onion, garlic powder, sugar, oyster sauce, light soy sauce, and black pepper. Stir-fry for 2 minutes.

3. Add the tapioca starch water and stir-fry for 2 minutes, or until the sauce thickens. Remove from heat and serve hot with jasmine rice.

Yield: 4 servings

Stir-fried Pork with Thai Basil (Moo Pad Horapha)

Thai basil, which has a sweet, anise-like flavor, can be eaten many different ways: fresh; in stir-fries; in noodle soup; or in curries.

4 tablespoons peanut oil
3 cloves garlic (minced)
1 pound pork loin (cut into bite-sized pieces)
2 cups sliced fresh white mushrooms
1 cup sliced green bell pepper
1 cup sliced yellow onion
½ cup Thai basil (bai horapha)
1 teaspoon garlic powder
1 tablespoon light soy sauce
⅓ cup oyster sauce
½ teaspoon black pepper
1 tablespoon fish sauce (nam pla)
1 tablespoon sugar
1 teaspoon minced fresh Thai chili (optional)
½ cup water

Thai basil (bai horapha)

1. Preheat a wok over high heat and add peanut oil, swirling to coat the entire surface. Heat oil for 1 minute and add the garlic, stir-frying for 30 seconds. Follow with the pork and stir-fry for 6-8 minutes, or until fully cooked.

2. Add mushrooms, green pepper, and onion and stir-fry for 3 minutes. Follow with Thai basil, garlic powder, light soy sauce, oyster sauce, black pepper, fish sauce, sugar, Thai chili, and water and stir-fry for 1-2 minutes. Remove from heat and serve hot with jasmine rice.

Yield: 4 servings

Stir-fried Pork with Peanut Curry Sauce
(Pra Rahm Long Song)

My cooking class students always laugh when I tell them that Thai people love to eat peanut butter, just not in sandwiches! We mostly eat it in curries, stir-fries, and dipping sauces. After learning to make this dish, many of my students tell me this is their new favorite way to eat peanut butter!

½ pound Chinese broccoli
2 tablespoons peanut oil
2 tablespoons finely-chopped shallot
2 cloves garlic (minced)
1 pound pork loin (cut into bite-sized pieces)
3 tablespoons red curry paste (see page 164 or use pre-made)
1 cup coconut milk
½ cup chunky peanut butter
¼ cup water
1 tablespoon sugar
3 tablespoons fish sauce (nam pla)
⅓ cup ground roasted peanuts

Note: Spinach can be substituted for Chinese brocolli in this recipe. Clean thoroughly and cook in boiling water for 2 minutes. Drain and set aside.

1. Fill a soup pot with water and bring to a boil. Wash the Chinese brocolli and remove the stem ends and hard outer skin. Cut the leaves into 1½ inch pieces and diagonally cut the stems into 1½ inch lengths (keep separate as they're added at different times). Cook the brocolli stems for 5 minutes, or until soft. Add the brocolli leaves and cook for 2 more minutes. Drain and set aside.

2. Heat a wok over medium-high heat and add peanut oil, swirling to coat the entire surface. Heat the oil for 1 minute and add the shallot and garlic, stir-frying for 1 minute, or until golden brown. Add the pork and red curry paste and stir-fry for 6-8 minutes, or until the pork is fully cooked.

3. Pour in the coconut milk and let boil for 1 minute. Follow with peanut butter, water, sugar, and fish sauce and stir-fry for 4 minutes, or until red oil droplets appear. Remove from heat.

4. To serve Pra Rahm Long Song, place Chinese brocolli on a serving platter (if it's cold, warm in microwave for 1-2 minutes). Top with Peanut Curry Pork and sprinkle with roasted ground peanuts. Serve hot with jasmine rice or steamed rice noodles.

Yield: 4 servings

Stir-fried Pork with Peanut Curry Sauce (Pra Rahm Long Song)
served with Chinese brocolli

Stir-fried Chicken with Cashew (Gai Pad Med Ma Muang)

Cashews are used in Thai cooking for snacks, salads, stir-fries, and desserts!

4 tablespoons peanut oil
3 cloves garlic (minced)
1 pound chicken breast (cut into bite-sized pieces)
1 cup sliced fresh white mushrooms
⅓ cup sliced yellow onion
½ cup sliced water chestnut
1½ teaspoons garlic powder
1 tablespoon light soy sauce
1 teaspoon black soy sauce
⅓ cup oyster sauce
1 teaspoon fish sauce (nam pla)
1 tablespoon rice cooking wine
1½ tablespoons sugar
½ teaspoon ground white pepper
½ teaspoon ground Thai chili
2 stalks green onion (cut into 1 inch lengths)
½ cup roasted cashew nuts

Note: This is a dry stir-fry, but if you would prefer to have sauce with this dish combine 1 teaspoon tapioca starch and ⅓ cup of water. Mix thoroughly and add before the green onion goes in, stir-frying for 1 minute.

1. Heat a wok over medium-high heat and add the peanut oil, swirling to coat the entire surface. Heat the oil for 1 minute and add the garlic, stir-frying for 1 minute, or until golden brown.

2. Raise the heat to high, add the chicken and stir-fry for 6-8 minutes, or until the chicken is fully cooked. Make a space in the middle of the wok by pushing the chicken to the side. Add the mushroom, onion, water chestnut, garlic powder, light soy sauce, black soy sauce, oyster sauce, fish sauce, rice cooking wine, sugar, white pepper, and Thai chili and stir-fry for 5 minutes.

3. Add green onion and stir-fry for 1 minute. Remove from heat and sprinkle with roasted cashew nuts. Serve hot with jasmine rice.

Yield: 4 servings

Stir-fried Chicken with Pea Pods (Gai Pad Tua-luntow)

Everyone loves pea pods and this stir-fry is a quick, easy way to enjoy them!

3 cloves garlic (minced)
½ teaspoon black pepper
1 teaspoon sea salt
1 tablespoon light soy sauce
1 pound chicken breast (cut into bite-sized pieces)
3 tablespoons peanut oil
½ pound pea pods (or snow peas; remove strings before using)
1 tablespoon sugar
¼ cup oyster sauce
1 teaspoon corn starch + ⅓ cup water (mix thoroughly)
1 large tomato (cut into 8 pieces)

1. Combine garlic, black pepper, salt, and light soy sauce in a bowl. Mix thoroughly and apply to the chicken as a marinade, then set aside.

2. Preheat a wok over medium-high heat and add peanut oil, swirling to coat the entire surface. Heat the oil for 1 minute and add the marinated chicken. Stir-fry for 6-8 minutes, or until fully cooked.

3. Add pea pods, sugar, and oyster sauce and stir-fry for 2 minutes. Pour in corn starch water and stir-fry for 2 minutes. Finally, add the tomato and stir-fry for 30 seconds. Remove from heat and serve hot with jasmine rice.

Yield: 4 servings

Chicken with Lemon Grass (Gai Tod Ta-krai)

Lemon grass is often used in big pieces for flavoring dishes, but for this recipe it's heavily bruised so it can be eaten with the chicken. Both the lemon grass and garlic become darkly carmelized and richly flavored during cooking!

2 stalks lemon grass
1 pound chicken thighs (boneless and skinless is preferred; wash thoroughly and cut thighs in half)
3 cloves garlic (minced)
¼ teaspoon freshly-ground black pepper
½ teaspoon ground Thai chili
2 tablespoons palm sugar
1 teaspoon sea salt
2 tablespoons fish sauce (nam pla)
4 tablespoons peanut oil

1. Cut off the woody tops and bottoms of the lemon grass. Remove the outer 2-3 layers of the stalk and cut the tender middle section into 1 inch lengths. Bruise the lemon grass by hitting it with the back of a Chinese cleaver or pound it in a mortar and pestle.

2. Combine bruised lemon grass, chicken thighs, garlic, black pepper, ground Thai chili, palm sugar, salt, and fish sauce in a bowl. Mix thoroughly and refrigerate for 1-2 hours.

3. Heat a wok over medium-high heat and add the peanut oil, swirling to coat the entire surface. Heat the oil for 1 minute and add the marinated chicken mixture. Stir-fry for 15 minutes (the chicken and sauce will thicken and become caramelized). Remove from heat and serve with cold cucumber slices, lettuce, and jasmine rice or sticky rice.

Yield: 4 servings

Chicken with Lemon Grass (Gai Tod Ta-krai)

Catfish with Holy Basil (Pla Duke Pad Phet Bai Grapow)

Holy basil (bai grapow) is a very peppery flavored basil that's delicious when stir-fried with catfish. If holy basil is not available, substitute with Thai basil.

10 fresh red Thai chilies
3 cloves garlic
3 medium-sized shallots (sliced)
2 tablespoons sliced lemon grass
2 tablespoons chopped galanga
¼ cup chopped coriander root (or ¼ cup chopped cilantro stem)
1 teaspoon freshly-ground white peppercorn
1 tablespoon shrimp paste (kapi)
4 tablespoons peanut oil
1 pound catfish fillets (cut into bite-sized pieces)
5 Thai eggplants (cut into quarters)
2 tablespoons shredded krachai (rhizome)
5 kaffir lime leaves (remove the center stem)
2 tablespoons palm sugar
1 teaspoon sea salt
½ cup half and half
½ cup water
2½ tablespoons fish sauce (nam pla)
⅓ cup holy basil (bai grapow)

1. In a mortar and pestle (or food processor), pound the Thai chili, garlic, shallot, lemon grass, galanga, coriander root, and peppercorn until it's mashed. Add the shrimp paste and mix until it turns to a paste.

2. Heat a non-stick frying pan over high heat and add the peanut oil, swirling to coat the entire surface. Heat the oil for 1 minute, add the curry paste mixture, and stir-fry for 2 minutes. Add the catfish pieces and stir-fry for 5 minutes.

3. Add Thai eggplant, krachai, lime leaves, palm sugar, and salt. Using a spatula, stir gently for 3 minutes. Finally, add half and half and water, cooking for 5 minutes, or until the Thai eggplant is soft (stir often to prevent burning). Stir in fish sauce and holy basil and cook for 1 minute. Remove from heat and serve hot with jasmine rice.

Yield: 4 servings

ingredients for Catfish with Holy Basil

Catfish with Holy Basil (Pla Duke Pad Phet Bai Grapow)

Stir-fries 139

Scallops in Choo Chee Sauce (Choo Chee Hoy Shell)

Choo Chee is a creamy curry that features the flavors of krachai and kaffir lime leaves!

2 tablespoons peanut oil
1 pound scallops
¼ cup red curry paste (see page 164 or use pre-made)
2 tablespoons sliced shallot
1 tablespoon shredded krachai (rhizome)
1 can coconut milk (13.5 ounces)
2 tablespoons palm sugar
2 tablespoons fish sauce (nam pla)
2 kaffir lime leaves (thinly-sliced)
⅓ cup Thai basil (bai horapha)
1 cayenne pepper (shredded; can substitute with any red pepper)

1. Heat a wok over high heat and add the peanut oil, swirling to coat the entire surface. Heat oil for 1 minute, add the scallops and pan-fry for 2 minutes, turning once with a spatula. Remove from pan and set aside.

2. Reduce heat to low and add the red curry paste, stir-frying for 30 seconds. Follow with the sliced shallots and shredded krachai and stir-fry for 30 seconds. Raise heat to medium-high and add the coconut milk and palm sugar. Let boil until red oil droplets appear, about 3-5 minutes. Add the scallops and fish sauce and simmer covered for 4 minutes (stir occasionally to prevent burning).

3. Stir in the lime leaves and Thai basil and remove from heat. Place on a serving platter and sprinkle with shredded cayenne pepper (or any red pepper). Serve hot with jasmine rice

Yield: 4 servings

Squid with Green Peppercorns (Pla Meuk Pad Prik Thai On)

Fresh green peppercorns can be difficult to find, but they're available frozen or in jars, and they really give this dish a special taste!

3 tablespoons peanut oil
1 tablespoon minced hot yellow chili pepper (can use yellow peppers such as hungarian wax, serrano, jalapeno, or guero)
2 tablespoons minced garlic
2 pounds squid (score and cut into bite-sized pieces; see note below)
2 tablespoons shredded krachai (rhizome)
5 kaffir lime leaves (remove center stem)
1 tablespoon light soy sauce
1 tablespoon fish sauce (nam pla)
3 tablespoons oyster sauce
1 tablespoon sugar
¼ teaspoon ground white pepper
2 stems green peppercorn (available frozen or in jar with stem-on)
⅓ cup Thai basil (bai horapha)

Note: Squid is scored with shallow cuts on the inside of the skin so that it has a nice pattern and curls up when it's cooked. See page 94 for a photo of squid that's been scored prior to cooking.

1. Heat a wok over medium-high heat and add peanut oil, swirling to coat the entire surface. Heat oil for 1 minute and add the yellow chili pepper and garlic. Stir-fry for 1 minute or until the garlic turns golden brown.

2. Add the squid, krachai, lime leaves, light soy sauce, fish sauce, oyster sauce, sugar, and ground white pepper and stir-fry for 4 minutes.

3. Add the green peppercorns and Thai basil and stir-fry for 1 minute. Remove from heat and serve hot with jasmine rice.

Yield: 4 servings

Stir-fried Prik King Curry with Seafood
(Prik King Pad Talay)

This is a famous Thai dish but the name is a bit of a puzzle; Prik King in Thai means chilies and ginger, though the dish doesn't contain any ginger!

5 dried red chilies
3 cloves garlic
2 tablespoons sliced lemon grass
1 small turmeric root (approximately 2 inch long root; or use 1 teaspoon turmeric powder)
1 tablespoon chopped galanga
3 kaffir lime leaves (minced)
1 tablespoon shrimp paste (kapi)
3 tablespoons peanut oil
½ pound scallops
½ pound shrimp (peeled and deveined, leave the tail on)
½ pound long beans (cut into 1½ inch lengths; can substitute green beans)
1½ tablespoons sugar
1½ tablespoons fish sauce (nam pla)
¼ teaspoon freshly-ground black pepper
⅓ cup water

Note: Prik king curry paste is available in Asian markets. If you prefer not to make your own curry paste, use 2 tablespoons of the pre-made paste and skip step 1 of the recipe.

1. To make the prik king paste, combine dried chilies, garlic, lemon grass, turmeric root (or powder), galanga, and lime leaves in a mortar and pestle (or food processor). Pound until it turns to a paste. Add the shrimp paste and mix thoroughly.

2. Heat a wok over medium-high heat and add the peanut oil, swirling to coat the entire surface. Heat the oil for 1 minute, add the prik king curry paste (from step 1), and stir-fry for 30 seconds. Follow with the scallops and stir-fry for 1 minute.

3. Add the shrimp, long beans, sugar, fish sauce, black pepper, and water and stir-fry for 5 minutes. Remove from heat and serve hot with jasmine rice.

Yield: 4 servings

Stir-fried Prik King Curry with Seafood (Prik King Pad Talay)

Cha-om Omelette (Kai Tod Cha-om)

Cha-om is a most unique vegetable, very bitter-tasting when eaten raw, but delicious when cooked in an egg omelette. Kai Tod Cha-om is a very popular dish in Thailand!

8 eggs
3 tablespoons fish sauce (nam pla)
⅓ cup sliced shallot
½ pound cha-om (remove the hard, woody stems; available fresh or frozen at Asian markets)
⅓ cup peanut oil

1. Beat the eggs and fish sauce in a bowl until thoroughly mixed. Add the shallot and cha-om leaves. Mix thoroughly and set aside.

2. Heat a non-stick fry pan (10 or 12 inch) over medium-high heat and add peanut oil, swirling to coat the entire surface. Heat the oil for 1 minute and pour in the cha-om egg mixture. Spread it around so the entire pan is covered. Cook for 4 minutes, then flip with a spatula and cook for another

4 minutes. Remove from heat and cut into 2 inch square pieces. Serve with Shrimp Paste Dipping Sauce (see below; optional) and jasmine rice.

Yield: 4 servings

Shrimp Paste Dipping Sauce (Nam Prik Kapi)

1 tablespoon shrimp paste (kapi)
6 fresh Thai chilies
2 cloves garlic
2 tablespoons lime juice
1 tablespoon sugar
1 tablespoon fish sauce (nam pla)

Wrap shrimp paste in aluminum foil and grill for 1-2 minutes over a burner set at low-medium heat. In a mortar and pestle, pound chilies and garlic together until finely mashed. Add shrimp paste and pound several times. Add lime juice, sugar, and fish sauce and mix thoroughly. Serve with fresh vegetables, steamed vegetables, fried eggs, or fish.

Cha-om Omelette up close

Water Spinach with Soyabean Sauce
(Pak Boong Fie Dang)

Pak Boong Fie Dang is a favorite dish in Thailand! Fie dang in Thai means hot, smoky fire and that's why the oil is heated until it starts smoking -- it adds a rich, smoky flavor to the pak boong!

1 pound water spinach (cut into 2 inch lengths)
1 tablespoon soyabean sauce (tow jiew in Thai)
2 tablespoons oyster sauce (vegetarian oyster sauce, which is available in some Asian markets, can be substituted if you prefer)
½ tablespoon sugar
3 fresh Thai chilies (bruised)
2 cloves garlic (minced)
3 tablespoons peanut oil

Note: Water spinach (pak boong) is available at many Asian markets and should be used quickly as it does not keep fresh for very long.

1. Place water spinach, soyabean sauce, oyster sauce, sugar, Thai chilies, and garlic in a bowl and set aside (do not mix the ingredients, they should go into the wok in this order).

2. Heat a wok over high heat and add the peanut oil, swirling to coat the entire surface. Heat the peanut oil for 2-3 minutes (or until it smokes) and then flip the ingredients from the mixing bowl directly into the wok (use oven mitts to protect your hands). Cover with a lid and cook for 2 minutes, without stirring. Remove the lid and stir-fry for 2 minutes. Remove from heat and serve with plain rice soup or jasmine rice.

Yield: 4 servings

Water Spinach in Soyabean Sauce
(Pak Boong Fie Dang)

Chive Flowers with Tofu

Chive flowers give a sweet, crunchy flavor to the fried tofu in this simple dish!

2 tablespoons peanut oil
1 package firm tofu (14 ounces, cut into square cubes)
3 cloves garlic (minced)
¼ pound chive flowers (trim off the bottoms and cut into 1 inch lengths; if chive flowers are not available, use regular chives or green onions)
¼ pound fresh bean sprouts
3 tablespoons mushroom soy sauce
½ teaspoon ground white pepper

1. Heat a non-stick fry pan over high heat and add the peanut oil, swirling to coat the entire surface. Heat oil for 1 minute and add the tofu cubes. Fry for 5 minutes or until golden brown, turning occasionally.

2. Add the garlic and stir-fry for 45 seconds. Move tofu to the side and add the chive flowers, stir-frying for 2 minutes. Follow with bean sprouts, mushroom soy sauce, and ground white pepper, stir-frying for 1 minute. Remove from heat and serve with jasmine rice or rice soup.

Yield: 4 servings

Drunken Noodle with Chicken (Kuay-tiaw Pad Kee Mao)

The noodles are drunk with flavor, but they will not make anyone drunk!

1 pound fresh wide rice noodle (pre-cut in strips ½ inch wide)
3 tablespoons sugar
2 tablespoons light soy sauce
1 teaspoon black soy sauce
1 teaspoon sesame oil
½ teaspoon sea salt
1 teaspoon ground Thai chili
2 tablespoons fish sauce
2 tablespoons rice cooking wine
4 tablespoons peanut oil
4 cloves garlic (minced)
2 tablespoons finely chopped shallot
1 pound chicken breast (cut into bite-sized pieces)
⅓ cup sliced yellow onion
1 egg
½ cup Thai basil (bai horapha)
1 medium-sized tomato (cut into quarters)

1. Remove noodles from bag and microwave for 3-5 minutes (covered with a wet paper towel). Separate the noodles into single strands and set aside in a covered container. In a small bowl, combine sugar, light soy sauce, black soy sauce, sesame oil, salt, Thai chili, fish sauce, and rice cooking wine.

2. Heat a frying pan over high heat and add the peanut oil, swirling to coat the entire surface. Heat the oil for 1 minute and add the garlic and shallots, stir-frying for 1 minute. Add the chicken and stir-fry for 6-8 minutes, or until fully cooked.

3. Add the onion, noodles, and the ingredients from step 1. Get the spatula under the noodles, lift them up, and flip them over (if you just stir with the spatula, the noodles will get broken). Continue flipping the noodles for 3-4 minutes. Make a space in the middle of the wok (by pushing the noodles out to the sides) and add the egg, stirring constantly until scrambled. Add the Thai basil and tomato and stir gently until the ingredients are mixed, about 1 minute. Remove from heat and serve hot.

Yield: 4 servings

Pad Thai with Chicken

Stir-fried rice noodles are easy to make if you know how to get the noodles moving around in your wok!

1⅓ tablespoons light soy sauce
2 teaspoons black soy sauce
½ cup sugar
2 teaspoons black pepper
2 tablespoons vinegar
1⅓ tablespoons garlic powder
5 tablespoons fish sauce
½ cup peanut oil
¼ cup minced shallot
1 pound chicken breast (cut into bite-sized pieces)
4 eggs
1 pound dried rice stick noodles (small size, approximately ⅛ th inch wide; soak in cold water at least 3-4 hours, do not drain before using)
8 stalks green onion (cut into 1½ inch lengths)
4 cups bean sprouts
1 tablespoon ground dried shrimp
1 tablespoon ground Thai chili (optional)
¼ cup ground roasted peanut
1-2 limes (cut into wedges)

Note: The best way to make Pad Thai is to use a non-stick wok or fry pan that's at least 12 inches in diameter. If using a smaller pan, make the dish in 2 batches (if the noodles are too crowded, they won't get evenly flavored). A pair of cooking chopsticks are highly recommended also.

1. Combine light soy sauce, black soy sauce, sugar, black pepper, vinegar, garlic powder, and fish sauce in a bowl. Mix thoroughly and set aside.

2. Heat a non-stick wok (or frying pan) over high heat and add peanut oil, swirling to coat the entire surface. Heat oil for 1 minute and add shallots, stir-frying for 1 minute, or until golden brown. Add the chicken and stir-fry for 8 minutes, or until fully cooked. Make a space in the middle of the wok (by pushing the chicken out to the sides) and add the eggs. Stir-fry for 3 minutes, or until the eggs are scrambled.

Crying Tiger

3. Add the rice noodles and the sauce mixture from step 1. Use chopsticks to stir the noodles and ingredients together. Get the spatula under the noodles, lift them up and flip them over (this will keep the noodles from breaking). Continue using the chopsticks and spatula, flipping and stirring the noodles for 6-8 minutes, or until they're soft.

4. Add the green onion and flip and stir for 2 minutes. Add the bean sprouts and stir constantly for 30 seconds. Turn off the heat and add the ground dried shrimp. Sprinkle Thai chili on top (if desired), and serve hot with ground peanuts, fresh lime wedges, fresh bean sprouts, chives, or green onions.

Yield: 6 servings

Pad Thai with Chicken

Isaan-style Noodles with Pork (Pad Mee Isaan)

4 tablespoons peanut oil
3 cloves garlic (minced)
2 tablespoons thinly-sliced shallot
1 pound pork loin (cut into bite-sized pieces)
1 teaspoon sea salt
1 pound fresh rice noodle (cut into 5 inch lengths)
3 tablespoons sugar
3 tablespoons black soy sauce
4 tablespoons fish sauce
½ teaspoon ground Thai chili
2 stalks green onion (cut into 1 inch lengths)
1 cup bean sprouts

1. Heat a wok over medium-high heat and add peanut oil, swirling to coat the entire surface. Heat oil for 1 minute and add the garlic and shallots. Stir-fry for 2 minutes. Add the pork and salt and stir-fry for 7-8 minutes.

2. Add fresh rice noodles, sugar, black soy sauce, fish sauce, and ground Thai chili. Stir-fry until the noodle is soft, approximately 5 minutes (if the noodle gets too dry, add ½ cup of water). Add green onion and bean sprouts and stir-fry for 2 more minutes. Remove from heat and serve hot.

Yield: 4 servings

Isaan-style Noodles (Pad Mee Isaan)

Silver Bean Thread Noodle with Seafood
(Pad Woon Sen Talay)

Pad Woon Sen differs from other stir-fried noodle dishes because it's usually served with rice!

3 tablespoons peanut oil
3 cloves garlic (minced)
½ pound shrimp
½ pound scallops
1 egg (beaten)
½ cup sliced yellow onion
¼ pound bok choy (cut into 1 inch lengths)
¼ pound silver bean thread noodle (soak in hot water until soft and drain)
1 medium-sized firm tomato (cut into 4 pieces)
1 tablespoon sugar
1 teaspoon garlic powder
½ teaspoon black pepper
3 tablespoons mushroom soy sauce
1 teaspoon sea salt
½ teaspoon ground Thai chili

1. Heat a wok over medium-high heat and pour in the peanut oil, swirling to coat the entire surface. Heat the oil for 1 minute and add the garlic, stir-frying until it's golden brown. Add the scallops and stir-fry for 1 minute. Add the shrimp and stir-fry for 2 more minutes.

2. Make a place in the middle of the wok (by pushing the shrimp and scallops to the sides) and add the beaten egg, stir-frying for 30 seconds. Raise the heat to high and add the onion and bok choy, stir-frying for 1 minute.

3. Add the bean thread noodle, tomato, sugar, garlic powder, black pepper, mushroom soy sauce, salt, and Thai chili and stir-fry for 2 minutes. Remove from heat and serve with jasmine rice.

Yield: 4 servings

Silver Bean Thread Noodle with Seafood (Pad Woon Sen Talay)

Wide Rice Noodle with Beef (Rad Na Nua)

Rad Na in Thai means a sauce or gravy poured over noodles.

3 cloves garlic (minced)
1 tablespoon light soy sauce
½ teaspoon white pepper
1 pound sirloin tip beef (cut into bite-sized pieces)
2 pounds fresh wide rice noodle (cut into 1 inch wide strips)
1 tablespoon black soy sauce
½ pound Chinese broccoli (called gai-lan in Cantonese or kana in Thai)
4 tablespoons peanut oil
1 teaspoon soyabean sauce (tow jiew in Thai)
⅓ cup oyster sauce
1½ tablespoons sugar
1 tablespoon vinegar
2 tablespoons corn starch + 1½ cups water (mixed)
¼ teaspoon ground Thai chili

Note: Fresh wide rice noodles, also called chow fun noodles, are sold in 1 or 2 pound packages in most Asian markets. The noodles can have a short shelf-life, so check the package to make sure there are no signs of mold.

1. Combine garlic, light soy sauce, and white pepper in a bowl and apply as a marinade to the beef. Set aside at room temperature until ready to use.

2. Microwave the rice noodles in wet paper towels for 5-6 minutes, or until soft. Pull apart the noodles so each layer is separate and color them with the black soy sauce. Set aside in a tight container to keep them moist.

3. Thoroughly rinse the Chinese brocolli and cut off the ends of the stems, as well as the hard outer skin. Cut in half so the leaves and stems are separate (they will go in at different times). Cut the leaves into 1½ inch pieces, and cut the stems diagonally into 1½ inch lengths.

3. Preheat a wok over high heat and add peanut oil, swirling to coat the entire surface. Heat oil for 1 minute and add the marinated beef, stir-frying for 4 minutes. Add the Chinese brocolli stems and stir-fry for 3 minutes. Follow with the soyabean sauce, oyster sauce, sugar, and vinegar, stir-frying for 1 minute. Add the Chinese brocolli leaves and stir-fry for 1-2 minutes.

4. Pour in the cornstarch water and stir-fry until the sauce thickens, about 2 minutes. Remove from heat and stir in ground Thai chili. Arrange the rice noodles on a plate and pour the sauce over it. This dish should be served hot.

Yield: 4 servings

Wide Rice Noodle with Beef (Rad Na Nua)

Rice Noodle with Black Soy (Pad See-iew)

Pad See-iew, along with Pad Thai and Rad Na, is one of the most popular dishes at noodle shops in Thailand!

1 teaspoon ground white pepper
2 tablespoons light soy sauce
4 cloves garlic (minced)
1 pound pork loin (cut into bite-sized pieces)
1 pound fresh wide rice noodle (pre-cut into ¼ inch strips; also called chow fun noodle)
3 tablespoons black soy sauce
½ pound Chinese brocolli
4 tablespoons peanut oil
2 eggs (scrambled)
1½ teaspoons sea salt
2 tablespoons sugar

1. Combine white pepper, light soy sauce, and garlic in a bowl and apply as a marinade to the pork. Set aside at room temperature until ready to use.

2. Microwave the noodles in wet paper towels for 3-5 minutes or until soft. Pull apart the noodles so each layer is separate and color with black soy sauce. Place in a covered container to keep moist and set aside.

3. Thoroughly wash the Chinese brocolli and remove the stem ends and hard outer skin. Cut the leaves into 1½ inch pieces and cut the stems diagonally into 1½ inch lengths (keep them separate as they're added at different times).

4. Heat a wok over high heat and add the peanut oil, swirling to coat the entire surface. Heat oil for 1 minute and add the marinated pork, stirring for 8 minutes. Add brocolli stems and stir-fry for 3 minutes. Add the rice noodles, brocolli leaves, scrambled eggs, salt, and sugar. Get the spatula under the noodles, lift them up, and flip them over (if you just stir with the spatula, the noodles will get broken). Continue to lift and flip the noodles for 5 minutes. Remove from heat and serve hot with Chili Vinegar (see opposite).

Yield: 4 servings

Chili Vinegar (Prik Dong)

2 tablespoons vinegar
2 fresh Thai chilies (sliced)

Mix ingredients thoroughly and serve with Pad See-iew, Rad Na, Noodle Soup (Kuay-tiaw), and Rice Soup with Pork.

Rice Noodle with Black Soy (Pad See-iew)

Rice Noodle with Catfish Curry (Kanom Jeen Numya Pla)

In Isaan, this noodle dish is not commonly sold in noodle shops! Instead, it's sold on the street by vendors selling Som Tum (Green Papaya Salad).

1 pound dried guilin noodle (small size)
4 cups water
1 stalk lemon grass (cut into 1 inch lengths)
3 slices galanga (⅛ th inch thick)
5 kaffir lime leaves
¼ pound ginger root (remove skin and cut into ⅛ th inch thick slices)
2 tablespoons shredded krachai
3 dried chili pop peppers (remove seeds)
3 medium-sized shallots
1 tablespoon sea salt
3 tablespoons fish sauce
1 pound catfish fillets
1 can coconut milk (13.5 ounces)
½ pound fresh bean sprouts
⅓ cup fresh lemon basil (bai maengluck; can substitute Thai basil)

Note: Krachai (also called rhizome) is available either frozen or in jars at Asian markets.

1. Fill a soup pot with water and bring to a boil. Add guilin noodle and cook for 3-5 minutes, or until soft. Drain in cold water and make little bundles out of the noodles. Cover with plastic wrap to keep moist and set aside.

2. In a soup pot, bring 4 cups of water to a boil. Add lemon grass, galanga, lime leaves, ginger, krachai, chili pop, shallot, salt, fish sauce, and catfish and cook for 5 minutes. Remove from heat and let cool.

3. Remove lemon grass, galanga, and lime leaves from the mixture and place the remainder, including the water, in a food processor (or blender). Mix the ingredients until they turn to a paste and set aside.

4. Skim off the coconut cream from the can of coconut milk and place in a soup pot. Bring to a boil and cook for 2 minutes. Add the paste from the food processor and cook until oil droplets appear, approximately 3-5 min-

utes. Pour in the rest of the coconut milk and cook for 3 more minutes, stirring occasionally. Remove from heat.

5. To serve, place several bundles of noodles on a plate and top with catfish curry, bean sprouts, and lemon basil (or Thai basil). Serve warm with lots of fresh vegetables, such as sliced green beans, sliced cabbage, and mint leaves.

Yield: 6 servings

Rice Noodle with Catfish Curry (Kanom Jeen Numya Pla)

Green Curry with Pork (Gang Kiowan Moo)

Green Curry with Pork is a favorite Thai dish and it can be served with kanom jeen noodles instead of rice if you prefer!

1 can coconut milk (13.5 ounces; do not shake the can)
⅓ cup green curry paste (see below or use pre-made)
1 pound boneless country-style pork ribs (cut into bite-sized pieces)
4 cups water
2 tablespoons palm sugar
5 kaffir lime leaves (remove stem)
3 tablespoons fish sauce
2 teaspoons sea salt
10 Thai eggplants (cut in half)
½ pound sugar snap peas or pea pods (remove strings)
½ cup Thai basil (bai horapha)

1. In a soup pot over medium-high heat, spoon out the thickest part of the coconut milk from the can (about ½ cup) and bring to a boil for 2 minutes. Add the green curry paste and stir-fry for 1 minute. Add the pork and stir-fry for 2 minutes.

2. Raise the heat to high and add the rest of the coconut milk, water, palm sugar, lime leaves, and salt. Let boil for 8 minutes, stirring occasionally. Reduce heat to medium and cook until the pork is tender, about 10-15 minutes.

3. Add Thai eggplant and cook for 4 minutes, stirring occasionally to prevent burning. Add sugar snap peas (or pea pods) and stir gently for 2 minutes. Turn off the heat and stir in the Thai basil. Serve hot with jasmine rice.

Yield: 4 servings

Green Curry Paste (Krueng Gang Kiowan)

1 teaspoon white peppercorn
1 teaspoon cumin seed
1 teaspoon coriander seed
2 tablespoons minced fresh green Thai chili (prik kee noo)

1 tablespoon minced lemon grass
2 tablespoons minced galanga
5 kaffir lime leaves (minced)
⅓ cup minced coriander root (or cilantro)
1 tablespoon shrimp paste (kapi)

Note: For a milder curry, substitute any mild green pepper instead of green Thai chili.

Wrap white peppercorn, cumin seed, and coriander seed in aluminum foil and roast over a burner at low heat for 1-2 minutes. In a mortar and pestle (or food processor), pound the white peppercorn, cumin seed, and coriander seed. Add the rest of the ingredients and pound into a paste. Will keep in the refrigerator for 2 weeks.

Green Curry with Pork (Gang Massamun Moo

Red Curry with Chicken (Gang Dang Gai)

Red curry paste gets it's color from red peppers; for a deeper red color, let the curry paste and coconut milk simmer longer.

1 can coconut milk (13.5 ounces; do not shake the can)
⅓ cup red curry paste (see below or use pre-made)
1 pound boneless skinless chicken thighs (cut into bite-sized pieces)
2 cups water
2 tablespoons palm sugar
2 teaspoons sea salt
1 cup sliced bamboo shoots (drain in hot water)
4 kaffir lime leaves
3 tablespoons fish sauce
½ cup Thai basil (bai horapha)

1. In a soup pot over medium-high heat, spoon out the thickest part of the coconut milk from the can (about ½ cup) and bring to a boil for 2 minutes. Add the red curry paste and stir-fry for 1 minute. Follow with the chicken and stir-fry for 3 minutes.

2. Raise the heat to high and add the rest of the coconut milk, water, palm sugar, salt, and bamboo shoots. Let boil for 8 minutes, stirring occasionally. Turn off the heat and stir in the Thai basil. Serve hot with jasmine rice.

Yield: 4 servings

Red Curry Paste (Krueng Gang Dang)

1 teaspoon coriander seed
1 teaspoon white peppercorn
15 dried Thai chilies (remove the seeds; substitute with red bell pepper or any mild red pepper for a less spicy curry)
2 tablespoons thinly-sliced lemon grass
2 tablespoons minced galanga
3 kaffir lime leaves (minced)
3 medium-sized shallots (sliced)
1 teaspoon sea salt

1 tablespoon shrimp paste (kapi)
2 cloves garlic (minced)
5 coriander roots (or ¼ cup chopped cilantro)

Wrap coriander seed and white peppercorn in aluminum foil and roast over a burner at low heat for 1-2 minutes. In a mortar and pestle (or food processor), pound the coriander seed and white peppercorn. Add the rest of the ingredients and pound into a paste. The paste will keep in the refrigerator for 2 weeks.

Red Curry with Chicken (Gang Dang Gai)

Massamun Curry with Beef (Gang Massamun Nua)

Massamun Curry features the flavors of India and Malaysia, as well as a beautiful golden brown color.

1 can coconut milk (13.5 ounces; do not shake the can)
⅓ cup massamun curry paste (see opposite, or use pre-made)
1 pound sirloin tip beef (cut into 2 inch square pieces)
5 bay leaves
2 tablespoons palm sugar
3 cardamom pods (optional; roast in 400 degree oven for 10 minutes)
1 cinnamon stick (optional; roast in 400 degree oven for 10 minutes)
3 tablespoons fish sauce
2 tablespoons tamarind concentrate
5 cups water
½ cup yellow onion (cut into squares)
5 medium-sized potatoes (boiled and cut into quarters)
½ cup roasted or boiled peanuts

Note: Cardamom pods are available at some Asian markets and most Indian markets.

1. In a soup pot over medium-high heat, spoon out the thickest part of the coconut milk from the can (about ½ cup) and bring to a boil for 2 minutes. Add the massamun curry paste and cook for 1 minute, stirring constantly to prevent burning. Add the beef and stir for 2 minutes.

2. Raise the heat to high and add the rest of the coconut milk, bay leaves, palm sugar, cardamom pods, cinnamon stick, fish sauce, tamarind concentrate, and water. Let boil for 8 minutes, stirring occasionally. Reduce heat to medium and cook until the beef is tender, about 20-30 minutes.

3. Add the onion and cooked potatoes and stir gently for 5 minutes. Stir in roasted (or boiled) peanuts, and turn off the heat. Remove cardamom pods and cinnamon stick before serving. Serve with jasmine rice, basmati rice, or french bread.

Yield: 4 servings

Massamun Curry Paste (Krueng Gang Massamun)

1 teaspoon white peppercorn
½ teaspoon cumin seed
2 cloves
1 teaspoon coriander seed
10 cloves garlic (peeled)
6 medium-sized shallots (peeled)
2 tablespoons thinly-sliced lemon grass
2 tablespoons minced galanga
1 tablespoon shrimp paste (kapi)
2 chili pop peppers (remove seeds and soak in warm water until soft)

1. Preheat oven to 400 degrees and place all the ingredients (except chili pop) in aluminum foil. Bake for 10 minutes, remove from heat and allow to cool.

2. In a mortar and pestle (or food processor), pound the white peppercorn, cumin seed, cloves, and coriander seed. Add the rest of the ingredients and pound into a paste. Will keep in the refrigerator for up to 2 weeks.

Massamun Curry with Beef (Gang Massamun Nua)

Pork with Yellow Curry (Gang Karee Moo)

Yellow curry powder adds both flavor and color to this delectable curry dish!

1 can coconut milk (13.5 ounces; do not shake the can)
⅓ cup karee curry paste (see below or use pre-made)
1 pound boneless country-style pork ribs (cut into 1 inch thick pieces)
4 bay leaves
3 tablespoons palm sugar
1 teaspoon sea salt
3 cups water
3 tablespoons fish sauce
1 medium-sized carrot (cut into 1 inch lengths and boiled)
1 medium-sized potato (cut into quarters and boiled)
2 tablespoons sliced shallot (fry in 2 tablespoons peanut oil until golden brown, or use pre-made fried shallot available at Asian markets)

1. In a soup pot over medium-high heat, spoon out the thickest part of the coconut milk from the can (about ½ cup) and bring to a boil, cooking for 2 minutes. Add the karee curry paste and stir-fry for 1 minute. Add the pork and stir-fry for 2 minutes.

2. Raise the heat to high and add the rest of the coconut milk, along with the bay leaves, palm sugar, salt, water, and fish sauce. Let boil for 8 minutes, stirring occasionally. Reduce heat to medium-high and cook until the pork is tender, about 15-20 minutes (stir occasionally to prevent burning).

3. Add cooked carrot and cooked potato and stir gently for 2 minutes. Remove from heat and sprinkle with fried shallot. Serve with jasmine rice and Ar Jard Sauce (see page 57).

Yield: 4 servings.

Yellow Curry Paste (Krueng Gang Karee)

2 medium-sized shallots (peeled)
5 cloves garlic (peeled)
1 tablespoon thinly-sliced lemon grass
1 tablespoon minced galanga
1 teaspoon cumin seed

1 teaspoon coriander seed
½ tablespoon shrimp paste (kapi)
5 dried Thai chilies
1½ tablespoons madras curry powder

1. Preheat oven to 400 degrees and place shallot, garlic, lemon grass, galanga, cumin seed, coriander seed, and shrimp paste on a tray. Roast for 10 minutes.

2. In a mortar and pestle (or food processor) pound the cumin seed, coriander seed, and dried Thai chili. Add the rest of the ingredients and pound until it turns to a paste. Will keep for up 2 weeks in the refrigerator.

Pork with Yellow Curry (Gang Karee Moo)

Isaan-style Beef Curry (Om Nua)

A Northeast Thai favorite, Om can contain many different veggies and herbs. This version features yu choy, dill, maengluck (lemon basil), lemon grass, galanga, and lime leaves.

1 pound beef sirloin (cut into bite-sized pieces)
2 tablespoons minced lemon grass
2 tablespoons minced shallot
2 tablespoons minced garlic
2 tablespoons minced galanga
10 fresh red Thai chilies (minced)
1 teaspoon sea salt
2 cups water
5 Thai eggplants (small size, cut in half)
5 kaffir lime leaves (remove stem)
2 stalks yu choy (cut into 1½ inch lengths)
2 stalks green onion (cut into 1½ inch lengths)
½ teaspoon shrimp paste (kapi)
1 tablespoon fish sauce
1 tablespoon fermented fish sauce (pla ra)
1 tablespoon roasted rice powder (see page 43 or use pre-made)
1 cup chopped dill
½ cup lemon basil (bai maengluck)

Note: Yu choy, as well as galanga, Thai eggplant, lime leaves, kapi, and pla ra, is available at most Asian markets.

1. In a soup pot, add the beef, lemon grass, shallot, garlic, galanga, Thai chilies, salt, and ⅓ cup of water. Bring to a boil and cook for 3 minutes, stirring occasionally to prevent burning.

2. Add Thai eggplant, lime leaves, and the rest of the water. Bring to a boil and cook for 5 minutes. Add yu choy, green onion, shrimp paste, fish sauce, fermented fish sauce, roasted rice powder, dill, and lemon basil, and cook for 2 minutes, stirring to mix. Turn off the heat and serve with sticky rice.

Yield: 4 servings

Isaan-style Beef Curry (Om Nua)

Isaan-style Bamboo Shoot Soup (Gang Naw Mai)

Gang Naw Mai is a thick soup from Isaan that highlights the flavors of bamboo shoots, asparagus, yanang leaves, kayang, and galanga.

1 can whole bamboo shoots (20 ounces)
2 cups water
¼ pound green pumpkin (peel skin, remove seeds, and cut into bite-sized pieces)
1 stalk lemon grass (cut into 1 inch lengths)
3 slices galanga (⅛th inch thick)
3 medium-sized shallots (minced)
1 teaspoon sea salt
5 medium-sized dried shiitake mushrooms (soak in hot water and cut into quarters)
1 can yanang leaves extract (14 ounces)
¼ pound asparagus (cut into 1 inch lengths)
3 fresh Thai chilies (bruised)
3 tablespoons fermented fish sauce (pla ra)
1 tablespoon sticky rice flour + ⅓ cup water (mix together)
⅓ cup chopped kayang (or lemon basil)

Note: Yanang leaves extract, as well as fermented fish sauce (pla ra), sticky rice flour, kayang, and lemon basil, is available at most Asian markets.

1. Clean the bamboo shoots, remove any hard, woody parts, and cut into thin slices. Boil in water for 5 minutes and drain.

2. In a soup pot, bring water to a boil. Add bamboo shoots, green pumpkin, lemon grass, galanga, shallot, salt, shiitake mushrooms, and yanang extract. Cook for 5 minutes.

3. Add asparagus, Thai chili, and fermented fish sauce (pla ra) and stir to mix, cooking for 2 minutes. Pour in the sticky rice flour water and stir gently, cooking for 2 more minutes. Finally, add kayang (or lemon basil) and stir gently for 30 seconds. Remove from heat and serve hot with sticky rice or jasmine rice.

Yield: 4 servings

Isaan-style Bamboo Shoot Soup (Gang Naw Mai)

Bitter Melon with Catfish (Gang Om Mara Pla Duke)

As the name implies, bitter melon is indeed very bitter when eaten raw. Cooking reduces much of the bitterness and the red curry paste and coconut milk add an interesting taste!

½ pound bitter melon
1 can coconut milk (13.5 ounces; do not shake the can)
3 tablespoons red curry paste (see page 164 or use pre-made)
1 pound catfish fillets (cut into 1 inch long pieces)
2 tablespoons palm sugar
1 teaspoon sea salt
2 tablespoons fish sauce
1 cup water
⅓ cup chopped Thai basil (bai horapha)

1. Fill a soup pot with water and bring to a boil. Cut the bitter melon in half, remove the seeds, and slice into ¼ inch wide pieces. Add bitter melon to boiling water and cook for 5 minutes. Drain and set aside.

2. In a soup pot over high heat, spoon out the thickest part of the coconut milk (about ½ cup) from the can and let boil for 2 minutes. Add the red curry paste and catfish and cook for 2 minutes, stirring gently to avoid breaking up the catfish pieces.

3. Add the rest of the coconut milk, along with the cooked bitter melon, palm sugar, salt, and fish sauce. Cook for 5 minutes, stirring occasionally. Reduce heat to medium-high and pour in the water. Cook for 10 more minutes, stirring occasionally. Finally, add Thai basil and stir gently to mix. Remove from heat and serve with jasmine rice.

Yield: 4 servings

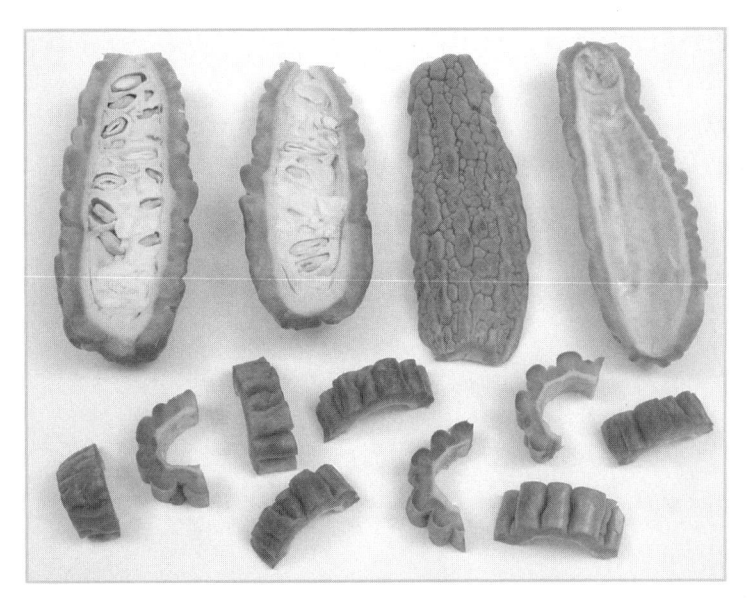

bitter melon

Bitter Melon with Catfish (Gang Om Mara Pla Duke)

Steamed Rainbow Trout with Young Ginger

The delicate flavor of rainbow trout is enhanced with young ginger, which has a very mild, subtle flavor (use regular ginger if it's not available).

1 pound whole rainbow trout (or fillets)
1 teaspoon light soy sauce
¼ teaspoon ground white pepper
2 tablespoons shredded young ginger
⅓ cup sliced dried shiitake mushrooms
(soak in hot water until soft)
1 cup white mushrooms (cut in half)
2 tablespoons oyster sauce
1 teaspoon soyabean sauce (tow jiew)
2 stalks green onion
(cut into 1 inch lengths)
1 tablespoon rice cooking wine
1 teaspoon sesame oil
water for steaming

young ginger

1. If using whole rainbow trout, gut the fish and wash thoroughly. Using a knife, make several shallow cuts in the skin (this allows the flavors to get into the fish). Combine rainbow trout (or fillets), light soy sauce, and ground white pepper in a bowl and mix thoroughly. Let marinate for 10 minutes.

2. Combine young ginger, shiitake mushrooms, white mushrooms, oyster sauce, soyabean sauce, green onion, rice cooking wine, and sesame oil in another bowl and mix thoroughly.

3. Bring water to a boil in a steamer. Place the marinated fish on a plate and cover with young ginger sauce (from step 2). Steam for 10 minutes. Serve hot with jasmine rice.

Yield: 2 servings

Steamed Rainbow Trout with Young Ginger

Steamed Seafood in Red Curry (Hor Moke Talay)

Traditionally, Hor Moke is steamed in banana leaves folded into little cups (see opposite). The leaves can be difficult to fold, but to get the same taste put a piece of banana leaf in the bottom of each ramekin (discard before serving).

2 tablespoons red curry paste (see page 164 or use pre-made)
1 egg
1 teaspoon sea salt
2 tablespoons fish sauce
½ cup coconut cream
¼ cup rice flour
¼ pound scallops
¼ pound shrimp (peeled and deveined, with tail removed)
1 pound red snapper fillets (cut into bite-sized pieces)
3 stalks green onion (cut into 1 inch lengths)
2 cups shredded cabbage
1 cup chopped Thai basil (bai horapha)
5 kaffir lime leaves (thinly-sliced)
⅓ cup shredded red bell pepper

1. Combine red curry paste, egg, salt, fish sauce, coconut cream, and rice flour in a bowl, mixing thoroughly. Add scallops, shrimp, red snapper, green onion, cabbage, Thai basil, and lime leaves (reserve 1 teaspoon for garnishing ramekins). Mix ingredients together very gently (to keep seafood from breaking apart) and set aside.

2. Bring water to a boil in a steamer. Scoop the fish and seafood mixture into 4-6 ramekins (4 inch diameter) and place on steamer shelves. Steam with cover on for 8 minutes. Top with coconut cream topping (see below), lime leaves, and red bell pepper and steam for 2 more minutes. Serve hot with jasmine rice.

Yield: 4 servings

Coconut Cream Topping for Hor Moke

⅓ cup coconut cream
1 teaspoon rice flour

Mix coconut cream and rice flour together and use to top Hor Moke.

Hor Moke Talay steamed in banana leaf cup

Steamed Seafood in Red Curry (Hor Moke Talay)

Fish & Seafood 179

Steamed Walleye with Vegetable (Pla Noong Pak)

When I was growing up, we ate steamed fish and vegetables nearly every day! Each morning the wives of local fishermen would walk through our neighborhood selling their husbands' catch, which usually included mudfish (the most similar to walleye), tilapia, or catfish. We always grew our own vegetables and quite often my dad and brothers went fishing and brought home a stringer of fish!

1 pound walleye fillets
3 tablespoons light soy sauce
1 teaspoon sea salt
1 stalk lemon grass (bruised and cut into 2 inch lengths)
½ medium-sized green pumpkin (wash and cut into 2 inch thick by 4 inch long pieces)
¼ pound Thai eggplant (cut in half)
¼ pound long beans (cut into 4 inch lengths; can substitute green beans)
½ cup lemon basil (bai maengluck)

1. Combine the walleye, light soy sauce, salt, and lemon grass in a bowl. Cover with plastic wrap and marinate in the refrigerator for 1 hour.

2. Bring water to a boil in the steamer and place the green pumpkin and Thai eggplant on the tray. Cover and steam for 10 minutes. Place the long beans, marinated walleye, lemon grass, and lemon basil on top of the pumpkin and eggplant and steam covered for 10 more minutes.

3. Using a spatula, carefully lift the fish and vegetables out of the steamer and place on a serving platter. Discard the lemon grass pieces and serve with sticky rice and Nam Prik Noom (see below).

Yield: 4 servings

Young Green Pepper Sauce (Nam Prik Noom)

10 young green cayenne peppers (can substitute banana peppers)
1 bulb garlic (remove skin)
5 medium-sized shallots (remove skin)
½ teaspoon sea salt

10 cherry tomatoes
2 tablespoons fish sauce
2 tablespoons lime juice
⅓ cup chopped cilantro

1. Preheat oven to 375 degrees and wrap cayenne pepper, garlic, shallot, and tomato in aluminum foil. Bake for 15 minutes and allow to cool.

2. In a mortar and pestle, combine pepper, shallot, garlic, and salt and pound until slightly mashed. Add tomato and pound several more times. Add fish sauce and lime juice and mix, followed by cilantro (the consistency should be similar to a thick salsa). If you do not have a mortar and pestle, chop the ingredients into small pieces and combine in a mixing bowl. Serve with barbecued meats, sticky rice, or steamed fish along with fresh vegetables such as green beans, cucumber, or lettuce.

Steamed Walleye with Vegetables (Pla Noong Pak)

Grilled Scallops in Banana Leaves (Ab Hoy Shell)

Scallops (hoy shell in Thai) are grilled in banana leaves in this recipe. Isaan people call the folded-up banana leaves Ab, which means container!

1 pound scallops
2 tablespoons thinly-sliced lemon grass
3 kaffir lime leaves (remove stem)
1 tablespoon sliced shallot
1 tablespoon minced garlic
1 tablespoon chopped red Thai chili
2 teaspoons sea salt
1 cup chopped dill
2 stalks green onion (cut into 1 inch lengths)
⅓ cup lemon basil (or chopped kayang)
4 banana leaves (cut into 10 by 10 inch squares)

1. In a mixing bowl, combine scallops and the rest of the ingredients (except banana leaves), and gently mix. Place 2 sheets of banana leaves together on a flat surface and put half of the mixture in the middle. Wrap it up into a square packet and use a toothpick to keep it together during grilling. Repeat for the other half of the mixture.

2. Grill the packets over charcoal at medium-high heat for 10 minutes (use a broiler if charcoal fire is not available, but cover with tin foil to prevent banana leaves from burning). Remove scallop mixture from the banana leaves and serve hot with sticky rice or jasmine rice.

Yield: 4 servings

Grilled Tilapia in Pandan Leaves (Pla Nin Pun Bai-toey)

Pandan leaves (bai-toey in Thai) are used in Thai cooking to impart a delicate aroma and flavor to food that's similar to that of roasted young coconut juice!

1 pound tilapia fillets (or fish of your choice)
1 teaspoon sea salt
1 teaspoon sesame oil
pandan leaves (available frozen at Asian markets; wash thoroughly before using)

1. In a mixing bowl, combine the tilapia fillets, salt, and sesame oil. Let marinate for 10 minutes.

2. Wrap tilapia fillets with pandan leaves (2 leaves per fillet). Cover with aluminum foil to keep the pandan flavor during cooking. Grill over medium-high heat for 5 minutes (charcoal fire or broiler). Remove foil and grill fillets for an additional 5 minutes.

3. Serve with Green Thai Chili and Garlic Sauce (see below), lettuce leaves, cilantro, and mint leaves.

Yield: 2 servings

Green Thai Chili and Garlic Sauce

5 fresh green Thai chilies
3 cloves garlic
2 teaspoons sugar
2 tablespoons chopped cilantro
2 tablespoons lime juice
2 tablespoons fish sauce

In a mortar and pestle, combine Thai chilies, garlic, and sugar and pound into very small pieces. Add cilantro, lime juice, and fish sauce and mix thoroughly. Serve as a dipping sauce with steamed or grilled fish or seafood.

Garlic and Pepper Pork (Moo Tod Kra-tiem Prik-tai)

Pork is the perfect meat for this dish as it complements the garlic and white pepper very nicely! Freshly ground white pepper will make the dish even more delicious!

1 pound pork loin (cut cross-wise into ¼ inch thick pieces)
2 tablespoons minced garlic
1 teaspoon ground white pepper
1 tablespoon soy sauce
½ teaspoon sea salt
1 tablespoon oyster sauce
1 tablespoon sugar
½ cup peanut oil for frying
lettuce leaves
cucumber slices

Note: Sriracha chili sauce is the perfect accompaniment to this dish; bottles of the sauce (imported from Thailand) are available in either strong, medium, or mild strengths at most Asian markets. Huy Fong, a brand that's made in America (with a rooster on the label) is also available and can be found at Asian markets and many supermarkets.

1. Combine pork loin, minced garlic, ground white pepper, soy sauce, salt, oyster sauce, and sugar in a bowl and mix thoroughly. Allow to marinate for at least 1 hour in the refrigerator.

2. Preheat a frying pan over high heat and add peanut oil. Heat oil for 2 minutes and place the marinated pork pieces in the pan. Cook for 10 minutes, turning once. Drain pork on paper towels and serve with jasmine rice or sticky rice, lettuce leaves, and cucumber slices.

Yield: 4 servings

Garlic and Pepper Pork (Moo Tod Kra-tiem Prik-tai)

Grilled Chicken (Gai Yang)

The scent of Gai Yang being grilled over charcoal wafts through many cities in Isaan! Restaurants selling Gai Yang always serve it with Som Tum (Green Papaya Salad) and Kao Niaw (sticky rice), in much the same way that hamburgers are always served with french fries in America!

2 pound chicken fryer (breast, drumstick, thigh and wing)
⅓ cup oyster sauce
6 cloves garlic (minced)
1 teaspoon black pepper
1 tablespoon soy sauce
1 tablespoon sugar
1 teaspoon sea salt
¼ cup minced lemon grass (optional)

1. Thoroughly wash the chicken and pat dry with a paper towel. Combine oyster sauce, garlic, black pepper, soy sauce, sugar, salt, and lemon grass (optional) in a bowl. Mix ingredients together thoroughly and apply as a marinade to the chicken. Refrigerate for at least 15-20 minutes.

2. Grill over charcoal at medium-high heat for 30-40 minutes, turning occasionally to prevent burning (if charcoal fire is not available, roast in 375 degree oven for 30-40 minutes).

3. Remove from grill and serve with chili sauce for chicken (available at Asian markets) or Gai Hor Bai-toey Sauce (see page 83), along with Green Papaya Salad (see page 84) and sticky rice (see page 116).

Yield: 4 servings

Grilled Chicken (Gai Yang)
served with Som Tum and Kao Niaw

Pan-fried & Grilled Meats

Crying Tiger (Sua Rong Hai)

The name of this famous Isaan dish is thought to have come from the stripes on the meat created by the grill, as well as the fact that the meat cries -- or drips -- when it's cut!

3 cloves garlic (minced)
½ teaspoon ground black pepper
3 tablespoons soy sauce
1 teaspoon sea salt
1 pound beef tenderloin or New York steak (¾ inch thick)

Note: A good quality cut of beef is highly recommended for this recipe. Crying Tiger should be served medium-rare, so a lesser cut of beef may not be tender and juicy after it's grilled.

1. Combine the garlic, black pepper, soy sauce, and salt in a bowl. Mix thoroughly and apply as a marinade to the beef (it works well to place the beef and all the ingredients in a plastic bag so it will be thoroughly coated). Refrigerate for at least 1 hour.

2. If barbecuing the beef, use a medium-hot fire and grill for 8-10 minutes, turning only once. The meat should be medium-rare when served, or no crying tiger! If using a broiler, keep the meat as far away as possible from the flame and broil for approximately 6-8 minutes, turning only once.

3. Cut the meat into thin slices and serve with Crying Tiger Sauce (see below), as well as lettuce, cucumber slices, mint leaves, and sticky rice.

Yield: 4 servings

Crying Tiger Sauce (Nam Jim Gaew)

1 teaspoon ground Thai chili
3 tablespoons soy sauce
1 tablespoon roasted rice powder (see page 88 or use pre-made)
1 teaspoon sugar
1 stalk green onion (thinly-sliced)

1 tablespoon thinly-sliced culantro (pak chee farang in Thai)
1 tablespoon lime juice

Mix all the ingredients together and serve with Crying Tiger or any grilled meats.

Crying Tiger (Sua Rong Hai)

Mango with Sticky Rice (Kao Niaw Ma Muang)

Sticky rice drenched with coconut milk is topped with fresh ripe mango slices in one of the all-time favorite Thai desserts!

1 cup coconut cream
½ cup sugar
½ teaspoon sea salt
3 cups cooked sticky rice (see page 116)
3 ripe mangos

1. In a saucepan over high heat, add the coconut cream, sugar, and salt. Bring to a boil and cook for 2 minutes, or until the sugar is dissolved. Add the cooked sticky rice and stir for 2 minutes. Remove from heat and place on a serving platter.

2. Peel the mangos and slice the fruit into long pieces. Place on top of the rice and serve warm.

Yield: 6 servings

Tapioca Combo Dessert (Ruam Mit)

Ruam Mit in Thai means friends gathering together, which is a good description for this dish -- many delicious ingredients combined together!

4 cups water
1½ cups sugar
4 pandan leaves (optional)
1 teaspoon sea salt
2 cobs sweet corn (remove kernels from cob)
2 cans coconut milk (13.5 ounces each)
1 can sugar palm seeds (23.6 ounces; also called attap, do not drain syrup)
1 package dried tapioca dice (3.5 ounces; soak in warm water for 3-4 hours)
1 package dried tapioca strips (7 ounces; soak in warm water for 3-4 hours)

1. In a soup pot, bring water, sugar, pandan leaves (optional), and salt to a boil and cook for 5 minutes. Add the sweet corn kernels and cook for an additional 5 minutes. Pour in coconut milk and allow to boil for 3 minutes. Remove from heat, pour in sugar palm seeds (with syrup), and set aside (if using pandan leaves, remove before combining with tapioca).

2. Fill a soup pot with water and bring to a boil. Add tapioca dice and cook for 30 seconds. Follow with tapioca strips and cook for 1 minute. Drain tapioca in cold water and combine with coconut milk mixture. Serve with ice cubes.

Yield: 8 servings

Yellow Mung Bean Dessert (Tao Suwan)

1½ cups dried yellow mung bean (soak in cold water overnight)
5 cups water
1 cup sugar
⅓ cup tapioca starch + ⅓ cup water (mix together)
1 cup coconut cream
½ teaspoon sea salt

1. Drain the mung beans in a colander. In a saucepan over high heat, add the mung beans and water. Bring to a boil and cook until the mung beans are soft, about 10-15 minutes.

2. Add the sugar and stir until it's dissolved. Follow with the tapioca water and stir constantly for 1-2 minutes, until the liquid thickens. Remove from heat and set aside.

3. In a saucepan, combine coconut cream and salt and bring to a boil, stirring constantly for 1 minute. To serve, ladle the mung bean mixture into a bowl and top with coconut cream. Serve warm or cold. Tao Suwan is traditionally served with Fried Bread Sticks (Patongo in Thai), which are available fresh or frozen at many Asian markets.

Yield: 4 servings

Banana in Coconut Milk (Kluay Buat Chee)

This delightful dessert can be made even tastier by using Thai bananas (kluay num wah). They're available in some Asian markets and should be used when they're medium-ripe, not soft!

½ cup brown sugar
2 pandan leaves (optional)
¼ teaspoon sea salt
3 cups water
1 cup coconut cream
2 pounds medium-ripe bananas (peel and cut into 4 pieces each)

1. In a sauce pan, combine brown sugar, pandan leaves, salt, and water. Bring to a boil and stir over medium-high heat until the brown sugar dissolves.

2. Pour in the coconut cream and stir for 2 minutes. Add banana slices and cook for 5 more minutes. Remove from heat and serve hot or cold (remove pandan leaves before serving).

Yield: 4 servings

Agar-agar with Coconut Cream (Woon Ka Ti)

Agar-agar is similar to jello, but is made from seaweed. It holds it's texture better than jello so it can be used to create objects with multi-colored layers!

Bottom Layer

2 tablespoons agar-agar powder
3 cups water
1 tablespoon vanilla sugar

1 cup sugar
4 drops food coloring (optional)

In a saucepan, add agar-agar powder and water, stirring to mix thoroughly. Bring to a boil and add vanilla sugar, sugar, and food coloring (optional), stirring until they dissolve. Remove from heat, transfer to an 8 x 8 inch baking pan or jello mold and allow to set.

Top Layer

1 tablespoon agar-agar powder
1 cup water
1 teaspoon vanilla sugar

½ cup sugar
½ teaspoon salt
1 can coconut cream (13.5 ounces)

In a saucepan, add agar-agar powder and water, stirring to mix thoroughly. Bring to a boil and add vanilla sugar, sugar, and salt, stirring until the sugars dissolve. Pour in coconut cream and stir for 2 minutes. Remove from heat and pour over the first layer. Allow to cool in the refrigerator. Cut into square pieces and serve cold.

Yield: 4 servings

Black Sticky Rice Dessert (Kao Niaw Dum Peiuk)

Black sticky rice is somewhat similar to wild rice, with a nutty flavor and a chewy texture. In Thailand, fruits such as lychee, longan, sugar palm seeds, and young coconut are often served with this dish, which resembles rice pudding!

½ cup coconut cream
1 teaspoon salt
5 cups water
½ cup sticky rice (soak together with black sticky rice in water overnight)
½ cup black sticky rice
1 cup sugar

1. Combine coconut cream and salt in a saucepan and cook over medium-high heat for 2 minutes, then set aside.

2. Drain both types of sticky rice and place in a soup pot, along with the water and bring to a boil. Cook for 10 minutes, stirring occasionally. Reduce heat to simmer and cook for 10-15 minutes, or until the rice thickens.

3. To serve, ladle rice into bowls and top with coconut cream. Serve warm or cold.

Yield: 6 servings

Grilled Yucca with Coconut Cream
(Mun Sum Pa Lung Ping)

Grilling is one of the very best ways to enjoy the sweet taste of the yucca root!

½ pound palm sugar (about 4 cubes or discs; see picture on page 42)
1 tablespoon vanilla sugar
4 cups water
1 cup coconut cream
1 tablespoon rice flour
½ teaspoon sea salt
1 pound yucca root (cut into 4 inch sections and remove the skin)

1. In a saucepan, add palm sugar, vanilla sugar, and water. Bring to a boil and cook until palm sugar turns to a syrup, approximately 10-15 minutes. Remove from heat and allow to cool.

2. In a saucepan, add coconut cream, rice flour, and salt. Boil for 2 minutes, stirring occasionally. Remove from heat and set aside.

3. Grill yucca over charcoal at medium-high heat for 30 minutes, turning occasionally to prevent burning (if charcoal grilling is not possible, bake in oven at 400 degrees for 30-45 minutes). Remove from grill and flatten the yucca with a rolling pin.

4. Dip yucca in syrup, place on a serving platter, and remove the inedible center stem. Top with coconut cream and serve warm.

Yield: 8 servings

Grilled Yucca with Coconut Cream (Mun Sum Pa Lung Ping)

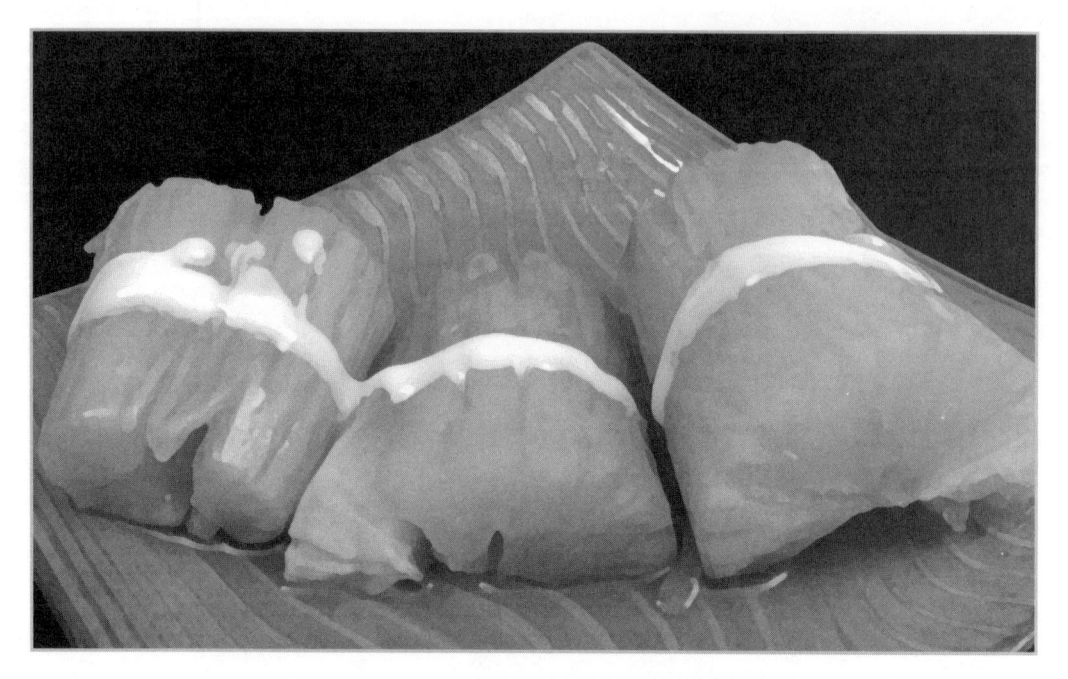

Sweet Yucca with Coconut Cream
(Cherm Mun Sum Pa Lung)

The rich, sweet taste of yucca root and coconut cream are combined to create a delicious dessert!

6 cups water
1½ cups sugar
1 pound yucca root (cut into 3-4 inch lengths and peel the skin)
1 cup coconut cream
½ teapoon salt

1. In a soup pot, bring water to a boil and add the sugar and peeled yucca. Cook until yucca turns soft, approximately 20 minutes. Remove from heat and place on a serving platter.

2. In a saucepan over medium-high heat, add the coconut cream and salt. Let boil for 1½ minutes, stirring occasionally. Remove from heat and pour over the cooked yucca. Serve warm or cold.

Yield: 6 servings

Baked Thai Custard (Kanom Mor Gang)

1 pound taro roots
5 eggs
¾ cup brown sugar
1 can coconut cream (13.5 ounces)
¾ teaspoon sea salt
2 tablespoons peanut oil
1 tablespoon thinly-sliced shallot

1. Peel the taro and boil for 5-10 minutes, or until soft. Mash thoroughly and set aside. In an electric mixer (or blender), add the taro, eggs, brown sugar, coconut cream, and salt. Mix for 2 minutes or until thoroughly combined.

2. In a saucepan over medium-high heat, cook the taro mixture for 5 minutes, stirring to prevent burning. Remove from heat. Preheat oven to 375 degrees. Place taro mixture in 8 x 8 inch pan or loaf pan and bake for 25-30 minutes. While it's baking, heat a wok with peanut oil over medium-high heat and add the shallot. Stir-fry until golden brown and set aside.

3. Remove custard from oven and poke with a toothpick to test if it's done (it should come out clean, if not bake for 5 more minutes). Sprinkle with fried shallot and allow to cool. Cut into slices and serve with hot Thai tea or coffee.

Yield: 8 servings

Boniato Ball Dessert (Kanom Kai Noke Gratah)

Boniato is similar to the potato, only much sweeter. In this recipe, boniato is mashed, made into small balls and deep-fried, much like little donuts!

¾ pound boniato (sweet potato)
1 cup sticky rice flour (glutinous rice flour)
1½ cup tapioca starch
¼ teaspoon baking powder
3 egg yolks (beaten)
⅓ cup sugar
⅓ cup coconut cream
peanut oil for deep-frying

Note: Boniato (sweet potato), along with sticky rice flour and tapioca starch, is available in many Asian markets (see page 36 for a photo of boniato).

1. Peel boniato and cut into small pieces. Boil for 15 minutes, or until soft. Remove from heat, drain, and mash (or use a food processor).

2. In a mixing bowl, combine sticky rice flour, tapioca starch, and baking powder and mix thoroughly, then set aside . In another mixing bowl, add the egg yolks, sugar, coconut cream, and mashed boniato and stir until it's thoroughly mixed. Add the sticky rice flour mixture and stir until everything's thoroughly combined.

3. Preheat peanut oil to 375 degrees in a deep-fryer or pan. Form boniato mixture into round balls, about 1 inch in diameter. Deep-fry until golden brown, approximately 5 minutes. Remove from oil with a wire strainer and drain on paper towels. Dust with cinnamon and sugar and serve immediately with hot coffee or tea.

Yield: 4 servings

Boniato Balls Dessert (Kanom Kai Noke Gratah)

Thai Cooking for Kids with Chef Tommy J.

I've been cooking since I was about 7 years old and I learned by watching my mom and grandma cook. It was my idea to have a kids section in this cookbook because I think that kids like Thai food and they might have fun making it themselves (with parental supervision, of course!)

Tom's Cooking Tips:

1. Always have a parent supervise your cooking!
2. Wash your hands before you cook and each time you handle meat!
3. Never wear loose-fitting clothing!
4. Be careful with knives (see step 1)!
5. Have oven mitts and potholders available!
6. Read instructions carefully!
7. Clean up your mess!
8. And most important......HAVE FUN!

[aroy dee in Thai means delicious!]

Tommy's Scrambled Eggs with Green Onion
serves 2

This was the first dish I ever cooked, and I still like it a lot (especially with jasmine rice!)

3 eggs
1 stalk green onion (chopped)
2 teaspoons fish sauce
2 tablespoons cooking oil

Combine eggs, green onion, and fish sauce in a bowl and beat until well mixed. In a frying pan (or wok) over medium-high heat, add the oil and heat for 1 minute. Stir in the egg mixture and cook for 2-3 minutes, flipping the eggs with a spatula once in a while. Remove from heat and serve with jasmine rice.

Thai French Fries, Onion Rings & Hot Dogs

5 medium-sized potatoes
1 large yellow onion
1 package hot dogs
3 tablespoons rice flour
3 tablespoons sticky rice flour
3 tablespoons tempura flour
½ cup water
oil for deep-frying

build a tower of onion rings!

1. Cut the potatoes into long strips (or use frozen pre-cut fries) and cut onion into thick slices. Cut hot dogs into 1 inch lengths and make ¼ inch cuts on each end (so it looks like an x; they'll puff up when they're deep-fried!). Combine 3 kinds of flour and water in a bowl and mix thoroughly.

2. Preheat oil in frying pan or deep-fryer to 375 degrees. Dip potatoes and onions in batter and deep-fry until golden brown (with parental supervision!) Deep-fry the hot dogs for about 45 seconds. Serve with ketchup (add a little sriracha chili sauce if you want it spicier).

[chicken in Thai is called gai and pork is called moo!]

Baked Chicken serves 4
Drummettes (Gai Ope)

1 pound chicken drummettes
(about 12 drummettes)
1 teaspoon garlic powder
½ teaspoon black pepper
2 tablespoons soy sauce
1 teaspoon sea salt
1 teaspoon sugar

1. In a mixing bowl, combine the chicken drummettes and the rest of the ingredients and mix thoroughly. Let chicken marinate for 15 minutes.

2. Preheat oven to 400 degrees. Place chicken on baking sheet and bake for approximately 20 minutes.

3. Remove from oven (with oven mitts) and serve hot with sticky rice or jasmine rice and chili sauce for chicken (available at Asian markets). If you want a spicier sauce, get a bottle of sriracha chili sauce at an Asian market!

Thai Cooking for Kids

Stir Fried Pork with Oyster Sauce and Tofu
serves 4

1 package firm tofu
½ pound cooked ground pork
¼ cup oyster sauce
1 tablespoon hoisin sauce
1 teaspoon sesame oil
1 teaspoon sugar
1 teaspoon sea salt
2 tablespoons peanut oil
1 cup diced yellow onion
⅓ cup diced green bell pepper

1. Drain and cut tofu into ½ inch cubes. Combine cooked ground pork, oyster sauce, hoisin sauce, sesame oil, sugar, and salt in a bowl and mix.

2. Heat peanut oil in a frying pan (or wok) for 1 minute and add onion and green bell pepper. Stir-fry for 2 minutes. Add the tofu cubes and the rest of the ingredients and stir-fry for 4 minutes. Remove from heat and serve with jasmine rice.

["kin kao, reu yang" in Thai means "have you eaten yet?"]

Thai Beef Jerky (Nua Tod)
serves 4

1 pound beef chuck roast
(cut into ½ inch thick slices)
1 teapoon black pepper
4 cloves garlic (minced)
3 tablespoons soy sauce
1 teaspoon sea salt
1 tablespoon sugar
2 tablespoons oyster sauce
oil for deep-frying

1. In a mixing bowl, combine the beef and the rest of the ingredients (except oil) and mix thoroughly. Place beef in the refrigerator to marinate for at least 30 minutes.

2. In a frying pan over medium-high heat, fry the beef for 6-8 minutes. Remove from oil and drain on paper towels. Serve with sriracha chili sauce and sticky rice or jasmine rice.

Beef and Potato with Oyster Sauce serves 4

4 medium-sized potatoes
3 tablespoons cooking oil
1 pound beef tip steak (thinly-sliced)
1 cup sliced yellow onion
¼ cup oyster sauce
1 tablespoon sugar
1 teaspoon sea salt
1 teaspoon corn starch
½ cup water

1. Wash the potatoes, cut into thin slices, and boil for 5 minutes to blanch them. Remove from water and drain.

2. Add oil to frying pan and brown potatoes for 3-4 minutes or until golden brown. Add the beef, onion, oyster sauce, sugar, and salt, and stir-fry for 6 minutes. Mix corn starch and water in a bowl and pour into frying pan. Stir-fry for 1 minute. Serve with jasmine rice.

[spicy in Thai is ped, wan is sweet, and prio is sour!]

Sticky Rice Dumplings
serves 4

½ cup sticky rice
½ pound ground pork
2 teaspoons sea salt
½ teaspoon black pepper
1 teaspoon sugar

An electric tabletop steamer (see left), available at many department stores, works great for steaming!

1. Soak sticky rice in warm water for 3 hours. Combine ground pork, salt, black pepper, and sugar in a bowl and mix thoroughly. Freeze for 15 minutes.

2. Make pork mixture into a ball (about 2 teaspoons) and repeat until all the mixture is used. Drain sticky rice and place on a plate. Roll the pork balls in the sticky rice until they're totally covered.

3. Steam in tabletop steamer (or regular steamer) for 10-15 minutes with the cover on. Remove from steamer and serve with soy sauce.

Thai Chow Mein (Goy See Mee) serves 4

4 ounces dried imitation egg noodle
¼ cup peanut oil
4 pieces baby corn (cut into small pieces)
2 ounces sugar snap peas or pea pods
(remove strings)
1 stalk green onion (cut into 1 inch lengths)
¼ teaspoon black pepper
1 teaspoon garlic powder
1 tablespoon sugar
1 tablespoon light soy sauce
1½ teaspoons sea salt
¼ pound chicken breast
1 teaspoon corn starch + 1 cup water (mixed)

1. Bring water to a boil in a soup pot and add the noodle. Cook for 4 minutes, drain in cold water and set aside. In a frying pan (or wok) over medium-high heat, add the oil and heat for 1 minute. Fry half of the noodle for 4-5 minutes or until golden brown. Remove from pan and drain on paper towels.

2. Using the same pan, cook the chicken for 4-5 minutes, or until thoroughly cooked. Add the rest of the ingredients (except the noodles) and stir-fry for 3 minutes. To serve, crumble the fried noodles on a plate and top with boiled noodles. Pour chow mein sauce over the noodles and serve hot!

In the Guinness Book of World Records, Bangkok (the capitol of Thailand) has the longest city name in the world! Here's a rough translation to English:

Krung Thep Mahanakhon Amon Rattanakosin Mahinthara Ayuthaya Mahadilok Phop Noppharat Ratchathani Burirom Udomratchaniwet Mahasathan Amon Piman Awatan Sathit Sakkathattiya Witsanukam Prasi

---

Fried Catfish serves 4
(Pla Duke Tod Grob)

8 ounces catfish (cut into ½ inch pieces)
2 tablespoons soy sauce
oil for deep frying
½ cup bread crumbs

1. Combine catfish and soy sauce in a bowl and refrigerate for 5-10 minutes.

2. In a frying pan over medium-high heat, add the oil and heat for 1-2 minutes. Cover the catfish with bread crumbs and deep-fry for 5-8 minutes, or until golden brown. Drain on paper towels and serve with jasmine rice or sticky rice.

Thai-style Udon Noodle Soup (Kao Pearng Sen) serves 4

To make the noodles:
1 cup rice flour
½ cup tapioca starch
¾ cup hot water

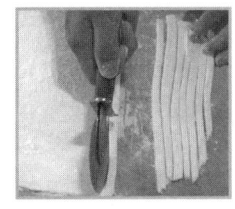

1. Combine rice flour and tapioca starch in a bowl and mix thoroughly. Gently pour hot water onto the flour and mix until it's thoroughly combined (if using an electric mixer, mix at high speed for 2-3 minutes). On a flat surface, dust with tapioca starch and flatten the flour mixture with a rolling pin. Cut into ¼ inch wide noodles (a pizza cutter works well).

2. Bring water to a boil in a soup pot and cook the noodles for 4-5 minutes (the noodles will float when they're done). Lift noodles out with strainer and set aside.

To make the soup:
4 cans chicken broth (or use homemade)
1 cooked chicken breast (shredded)
1 stalk green onion (sliced)
¼ cup sliced cilantro
1 teaspoon fried garlic (optional)
1 teaspoon sea salt
½ teaspoon black pepper

In a soup pot, add the chicken broth and bring to a boil. Stir in the cooked chicken, the noodles, and the rest of the ingredients and ladle into bowls.

[plate in Thai is jarn and bowl is toey!]

Veggie Combo (Pad Pak Roum) serves 4

3 tablespoons cooking oil
2 ounces cauliflower (cut into small pieces)
4 pieces baby carrot (cut into small pieces)
2 ounces brocolli (cut into small pieces)
2 ounces green beans (cut into small pieces)
⅓ cup sliced yellow onion
2 tablespoons oyster sauce
½ teaspoon black pepper
2 teaspoons sugar
1 teaspoon tapioca starch + ½ cup water (mix together)
½ teaspoon salt (optional -- add ½ teaspoon garlic powder)

Heat oil in wok and add cauliflower and carrot and stir-fry for 2 minutes. Add brocolli and stir-fry for 1 minute. Add the rest of the ingredients and stir-fry for 4 minutes. Remove from heat and serve with jasmine rice.

Condominium
(multi-layered dessert)

This dessert apparently got it's name because it can be made to look like a tall building if you make enough layers!

2 cups sugar
1 cup water
2 cups tapioca starch
¾ cup rice flour
1 teaspoon sea salt
1 can coconut cream
¼ teaspoon food coloring of your choice
1 teaspoon sea salt

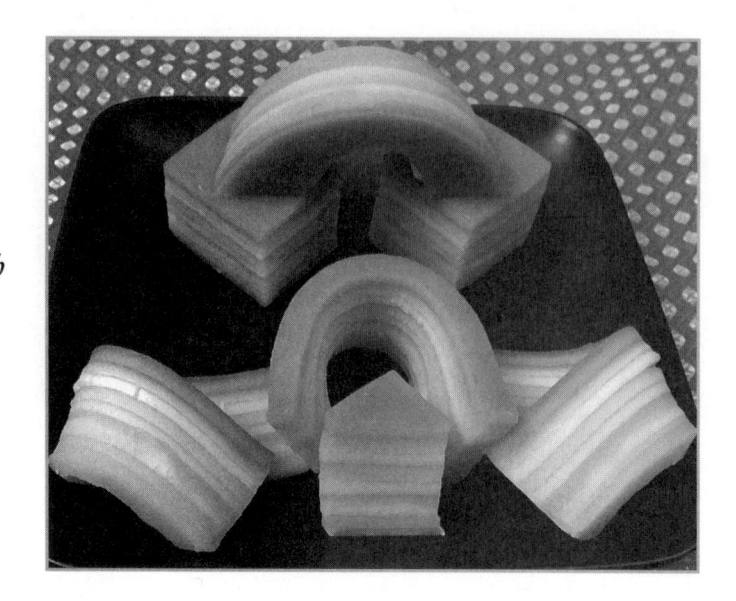

1. Combine sugar and water in a pan and boil for 10 minutes, then set aside. Combine tapioca starch, rice flour, and salt in a bowl and mix thoroughly. Add coconut cream and sugar water syrup and mix.

2. Divide into 2 containers and color each with food coloring of your choice. Using an electric tabletop steamer, pour enough batter into pan to make ¼ inch layer. Let steam for 5 minutes and then pour 2nd color on top. Repeat until you get to 5th or 6th layer (you should increase steaming time to 7 or 8 minutes per layer). To test each layer, place a clean finger on the top of the layer, if your finger sticks, it needs to steam longer. To serve, cut into slices or create your own design!

[spoon in Thai is chon, fork is chon som and knife is meed]

Thai Shaved Ice

Kids in Thailand love shaved ice, which is sold by vendors on the street!

You can make shaved ice in a blender or you can buy an ice shaver. Syrups from Thailand are available at Asian markets in flavors like strawberry, cherry, vanilla cream, and jasmine.

In Thailand, they also pour condensed milk over shaved ice, so you can try that if you like or you can use half and half or cream if you prefer!

Thai Pancakes (Kanom Kroke)
serves 4

1 cup rice flour
½ cup tempura flour
1 cup coconut cream
1 cup water
⅓ cup sugar
1 teaspoon sea salt
1 stalk green onion (sliced; optional)

Combine all the ingredients in a bowl and mix thoroughly. Spray Danish cake pan with cooking spray and heat over medium heat for 1 minute. Fill each one with batter. Cover and cook for 3-5 minutes. Remove the cover and cook for 2 more minutes. Serve warm.

If you don't have a Danish cake pan (also called an Aebleskiver), you can use a regular muffin pan and bake the pancakes in a 375 degree oven for 30-40 minutes.

[hiew in Thai means hungry and imm means full]

Floating Balloons Dessert (Bua Loy) serves 4

(I thought floating balloons would be a good name for this dish!)

1 cup sticky rice flour
2¼ cups water
1 cup coconut milk
½ cup sugar
½ teaspoon sea salt
water for boiling

1. In a mixing bowl, combine sticky rice flour and ¾ cup of water. Mix thoroughly and roll into small balls, ½ inch in diameter.

2. In a soup pot, get water boiling. Meanwhile, in another soup pot, add 1½ cups water, sugar, and salt and bring to a boil, stirring until the sugar dissolves. Add the coconut cream and let boil for 1 minute, then remove from heat. Drop the balls into the first pot and boil for 4 minutes (when coooked the balls will float). Lift the balls out with a strainer, transfer to the second pot, and stir gently to mix. Serve warm.

Thai Cooking for Kids

Online sources for Thai ingredients and equipment

http://www.importfood.com
www.importfood.com and www.thaigrocer.com are now the same company. They offer a large number of Thai cooking ingredients, including fresh lime leaves. They also offer a variety of cooking equipment including granite and ceramic mortar and pestles, 3 tray aluminum steamer, Thai pancake grill, hot pots, and sticky rice steamers and baskets.

http://www.templeofthai.com
www.templeofthai.com offers sticky rice bamboo steamers, hot pots, fresh kaffir limes and lime leaves, fresh galanga, fresh Thai chili (prik kee noo), and lots of dry products.

http://www.bangkokmarket.com
www.bangkokmarket.com offers a ceramic mortar and pestle, woks, wok tools, sticky rice steamer and basket and a sticky rice serving basket, as well as a large number of ingredients used in Thai cooking.

http://www.quickspice.com
www.quickspice.com offers rice cookers and bamboo steamers with a few other Thai cooking ingredients. It's primarily a Japanese and Chinese site.

http://www.thecmccompany.com
www.thecmccompany.com offers granite mortar and pestles, as well as dried Thai basil and dried Thai holy basil.

http://www.asianwok.com
www.asianwok.com offers a wok set, wire strainer, a small marble mortar and pestle and a wooden or stainless steel spatula.

http://www.i-clipse.com
www.i-clipse.com is the home of Pacific Rim gourmet. They offer fresh Thai basil, fresh lime leaves, fresh galanga, fresh turmeric, fresh banana blossom and frozen banana leaves. In addition to fresh produce, they offer mortar and pestles, rice steamers, sticky rice steamers and baskets.

http://www.globalfoodcompany.com
www.globalfoodcompany.com offers dried black and dried shiitake mushrooms, as well as canned straw and abalone mushrooms.

INDEX

agar-agar 43
Agar-agar with Coconut Cream (Woon Ka Thi) 194
Ar Jard Sauce 57
Asian chives 31

baby bok choy 32
bai grapow 18
bai makrut 19
bai-toey 35
Baked Chicken Drummettes 203
Baked Thai Custard (Kanom Mor Gang) 199
bamboo shoots 30
bamboo steamer 46
Banana in Coconut Milk (Kluay Buat Chee) 193
banana leaves 35
banana pepper 21
bean sprouts 30
Beef Bone Soup Broth 113
Beef Jerky 204
bitter leaf 33
bitter melon 28
Bitter Melon with Catfish (Gang Om Mara) 174
black fungus mushrooms 44
black soy sauce 40
Black Sticky Rice Dessert (Kao Niaw Dum) 195
boniato 36
Boniato Ball Dessert 200

carving knife 47
Catfish with Holy Basil (Pla Duke Pad Phet) 138
cha-om 34
Cha-om Omelette (Kai Tod Cha-om) 144
cha-ploo 33
chefs knife 47
cherry eggplant 23
Chicken and Coconut Soup (Tom Kha Gai) 104
Chicken and Rice with Ginger Sauce (Kao Mun Gai) 122
Chicken Bone Soup Broth 112
Chicken in Pandan Leaves (Gai Hor Bai-toey) 82
Chicken with Lemon Grass (Gai Tod Ta-krai) 136
chili pop 21
Chinese brocolli 25
Chinese celery 29
chive flowers 31
Chive Flowers with Tofu 148
chow fun noodles 38
cilantro 20
cinnamon stick 43
clay pot 48
Clear Noodle Soup with Tofu (Gang Jeud) 106
coconut 27
coconut cream 41

coconut milk 41
coconut sugar 43
Condominium dessert 208
cooking chopsticks 47
Crab Roll (Hoy Jaw) 81
Crispy Catfish with Green Mango 96
Crispy Rice Noodle (Mee Grob) 66
Crispy Sarong Appetizer 74
Crying Tiger (Sua Rong Hai) 188
culantro 20
curry paste 40
Curry Puff 72

daikon radish 28
dill 30
dried red chili 21
dried shrimp 43
Drunken Noodle with Chicken (Pad Kee Mao) 149

edamame 31
egg roll wrappers 43
Egg Rolls with Pork (Paw Piah Tod) 52

fermented fish sauce (pla ra) 40
fish sauce (nam pla) 40
French Fries 203
fresh rice stick noodle 38
Fried Catfish 205
Fried Chicken Wings (Peek Gai Tod) 78
Fried Rice Cake with Red Curry (Nam Kluke) 124
Fried Rice with Pork (Kao Pad Moo) 117
Fried Wonton with Pork (Giow Grop) 68
fuzzy squash 26

Gai Hor Bai-toey 82
Gai Yang 18
galanga 24
Gang Dang 164
Gang Jeud 106
Gang Kiowan 162
Gang Massamun 166
Gang Naw Mai 172
Gang Som 107
Garlic and Pepper Pork 184
ginger 24
glutinous rice flour 43
Green Curry Paste (Krueng Gang Kiowan) 163
Green Curry with Pork (Gang Kiowan Moo) 162
green mango 22
green papaya 22
Green Papaya Salad (Som Tum Thai) 84
green pumpkin 28
Grilled Chicken (Gai Yang) 186
Grilled Salmon Salad (Laab Pla Salmon) 90
Grilled Scallops in Banana Leaves 182
Grilled Tilapia in Pandan Leaves 183
Grilled Yucca with Coconut Cream 196

Index 211

ground Thai chili 41
guilin rice noodle 39

holy basil 18
Hor Moke 178
horapha 18
Hot Dogs 203
hot pot 45

imitation egg noodle 39
Isaan Bamboo Shoot Soup (Gang Naw Mai) 172
Isaan-style Beef Curry (Om Nua) 170
Isaan-Style Chicken Salad (Laab Gai) 88
Isaan-Style Noodles with Pork (Pad Mee Isaan) 152
Isaan-Style Papaya Salad (Som Tum Pla Ra) 86

Jasmine Rice (Kao Homm Mali) 116
jicama 37

kaffir lime leaves 19
Kanom Jeen Numya Pla 160
Kanom Kroke 209
kao kua 43
Kao Niaw 116
kapi 41
kayang 33
kowtong 33
kra-chet 32
kra-tin 34
krachai 24
Kuay-tiaw 100

Laab 88
lemon basil 18
lemon grass 19
Lemon Grass Salad (Yum Ta-krai) 98
light soy sauce 40
lime leaves 19
long beans 22
loofa gourd 26
lotus root 29
lin fah 33

madras curry powder 41
maengluck 18
makeua 23
malagaw 22
Mango with Sticky Rice 190
Massamun Curry Paste 167
Massamun Curry with Beef 166
Mieng Kham & Sauce 60
Mieng Kham 60
mint 19
mortar and pestle 45
mushroom soy sauce 40
mustard green 25

nam pla 40
Nam Prik Kapi 145
nam prik pow 41
Nam Soad 93
Nam Toke 99
Noodle Soup with Beef (Kuay-tiaw) 100
Nua Tod 204

Onion Rings 203
opo squash 26
oyster mushrooms 44
oyster sauce 40

pac peow 20
Pad Kee Mao 149
Pad See-iew 158
Pad Thai with Chicken 150
Pad Woon Sen 154
pak boong 33
pak chee 20
pak chee farang 20
palm sugar 43
pandan leaves 35
pea tips 31
peeler 47
peppercorns 41
Pineapple Fried Rice with Shrimp 118
Pla Noong 180
pla ra 40
plantain banana 37
Pork Bone Soup Broth 113
Pork Salad with Ginger (Nam Sod) 93
Pork Satay with Peanut Curry Sauce 56
Pork Toast (Kanom Punk Na Moo) 80
Pork with Yellow Curry (Gang Karee Moo) 168
Pra Rahm Long Song 132
prik kee noo 21
prik noom 21
puffball mushrooms 44
Pumpkin Coconut Soup (Fak Tong Gang Ka Ti) 110
purple eggplant 23

Rad Na 156
Rama Thai Pork 132
Red Curry Paste (Krueng Gang Dang) 165
Red Curry with Chicken (Gang Dang Gai) 164
rhizome 24
rice cooker 48
rice flour 43
Rice Noodle with Black Soy (Pad See-iew) 158
Rice Noodle with Catfish Curry (Kanom Jeen Numya Pla) 160
Rice Soup with Pork (Kao Tom Moo) 111
roasted rice powder 43
Ruam Mit 191

sadao 34

Sakoo Sai Moo, 58
Sarong 74
Sauce for Spring Roll 55
Scallops in Choo Chee Sauce 140
Scrambled Eggs with Green Onion 202
sea salt 41
sen mee 39
shallot 29
Shaved Ice 208
shiitake mushrooms 44
shredder 47
Shrimp on Lemon Grass Skewers 64
shrimp paste 41
Shrimp Paste Dipping Sauce (Nam Prik Kapi) 145
silver bean thread noodle 38
Silver Bean Thread Salad (Yum Woon Sen) 92
Silver Bean Thread Noodle with Seafood (Pad Woon Sen Talay) 154
Som Tum 84
Son-in-Law Eggs (Kai Luke Koei) 70
Sour Curry Soup with Shrimp (Gang Som) 108
Sour Curry Paste (Krueng Gang Som) 109
 soybeans (edible) 31
soy sauce 40
soyabean sauce with chili 41
spatula 47
spring roll wrappers 43
Squid Salad (Yum Pla Meuk) 94
Squid with Green Peppercorns (Pad Cha) 141
sriracha chili sauce 41
star anise 43
Steamed Rainbow Trout with Young Ginger 176
Steamed Seafood in Red Curry (Hor Moke) 178
Steamed Walleye with Vegetable (Pla Noong) 180
Sticky Rice (Kao Niaw) 116
sticky rice basket 48
sticky rice flour 43
sticky rice steamer 46
Stir-fried Beef with Holy Basil 126
Stir-fried Chicken with Peapods 135
Stir-fried Chicken with Cashew 134
Stir-fried Pork with Ginger (Moo Pad King) 130
Stir-fried Pork with Oyster Sauce and Tofu 204
Stir-fried Pork with Peanut Curry Sauce (Pra Rahm Long Song) 132
Stir-fried Pork with Thai Basil 131
Stir-fried Prik KIng Curry with Seafood 142
Stir-fried Sweet and Sour Pork 128
strainer 47
straw mushrooms 44
Stuffed Chicken Wings (Peek Gai Yod Sai) 79
Sua Rong Hai 188
sugar cane 37
Sweet & Sour Sauce for Egg Roll 53
Sweet Yucca with Coconut Cream 198

ta-krai 19

tamarind 35
tamarind concentrate 43
Tamarind Peanut Sauce for Lettuce Wraps 63
Tapioca Combo Dessert (Ruam Mit) 191
Tapioca Dumpling with Pork (Sakoo Sai Moo) 58
tapioca starch 43
taro root 36
Thai basil 18
Thai Beef Jerky 204
Thai chili 21
Thai eggplant 23
Thai Fish Cakes (Tod Mun Pla) 76
Thai French fries 203
Thai Hot and Sour Shrimp Soup (Tom Yum) 102
Thai Hot Dogs 203
Thai Lettuce Wraps (Pae Za Pun) 62
Thai Onion Rings 203
Thai Pancake 209
Thai Spring Rolls (Paw Piah Soad) 54
Thai Udon Noodle Soup 206
three tray steamer 46
Tod Mun, 76
Tom Kha Gai 102
Tom Yum Goong 102
tua ngok 30
turmeric 24

Udon Noodle Soup 206

Veggie Stir-fry 206

water mimosa 32
water spinach 32
Water Spinach with Soyabean Sauce (Pak Boong Fie Dang) 146
Waterfall Grilled Pork Salad (Moo Nam Toke) 99
Wide Rice Noodle with Beef (Rad Na Nua) 156
wing bean 34
wok 45
Wonton Dipping Sauce 68
Wonton Soup with Pork (Gio Nam Moo) 107
wood ear mushrooms 44

Yellow Curry Fried Rice with Shrimp (Kao Pad) 120
Yellow Curry Paste (Krueng Gang Karee) 169
yellow curry powder 41
Yellow Mung Bean Dessert (Dao Suwan) 192
yellow soyabean sauce 41
young green coconut 27
young green pepper 21
Young Green Pepper Sauce (Nam Prik Noom) 181
yu choy 25
yucca root 36
Yum Pla Duke Foo 96
Yum Pla Meuk 94
Yum Woon Sen 92